BEYOND HUNTING AND FISHING

The Last Experiences and Other Thoughts by a Guy Who Couldn't Quit

BEN D. MAHAFFEY

iUniverse, Inc.
Bloomington

Beyond Hunting and Fishing
The Last Experiences and Other Thoughts by a Guy Who Couldn't Quit

Copyright © 2012 Ben D. Mahaffey

iUniverse books may be ordered through booksellers or by contacting:

iUniverse
1663 Liberty Drive
Bloomington, IN 47403
www.iuniverse.com
1-800-Authors (1-800-288-4677)

ISBN: 978-1-4697-8936-1 (sc)
ISBN: 978-1-4697-8937-8 (e)

Printed in the United States of America

iUniverse rev. date: 3/31/2012

Contents

Attitude of Gratitude

Of my many weaknesses and imperfections, gratitude and appreciation are not included; at least I'm hopeful of acknowledging and showing appreciation. What accomplishments I've made, are mostly the result of the influence, guidance and teachings of so many people. To list them would be impossible, of course. There have been so many during a life span of 80 years.

Charles Swindoll, author, educator and Christian Pastor said: *"Attitude, to me, is more important than the past; than money; than circumstances; than failures; than success; than what other people think or say or do. It is more important than appearance, giftedness, or skill. It will make or break a company, a church, a home. The remarkable thing is we have a choice every day, regarding the attitude we will embrace for that day."*

At any given time in our lives, we are the product of the sum of all of our experiences and our responses to those experiences; this includes those that are positive and negative. Fortune has smiled upon me by having been born in the greatest period of time in the history of this planet; an American, with all of the benefits that have been earned by the blood and sacrifice of millions of people in my behalf, as well as my Savior Jesus Christ.

This fifth and final volume of various experiences and philosophies has been made possible by the above conditions. It has been written with the deep gratitude for all who have contributed to my being … pioneers, entrepreneurs, educators, doctors, church leaders, personal family and the human family, all receive my appreciation and devotion.

Introduction

Charles Dickens, in the early 19th Century, coined the famous statement concerning England, in his timeless novel, A TALE OF TWO CITIES. This condition could be today, as well as other times in the past.

"It was the best of times, it was the worst of times, it was the age of wisdom, it was the age of foolishness, it was the epoch of belief, it was the epoch of incredulity, it was the season of Light, it was the season of Darkness, it was the spring of hope, it was the winter of despair, we had everything before us, we had nothing before us."

As we sail the seas of life, we often have these feelings. Mankind has been subjected to every type of challenge and yet survives. During the German bombing blitz of England in September of 1940, a poster was created. It had a red background with a crown at the top. Its capital letters in white carried a simple message: KEEP CALM AND CARRY ON.

This latest book, and probably the last that I write, has been written with that concept in mind. Conditions in the world today could cause one to continuously wring his hands. And so the content varies greatly from the short stories in the other books. This writing contains other accounts that I have felt were worth reading, not necessarily because they are my stories, but because they relate to other themes in addition to hunting and fishing: politics, religion, war stories and philosophy. In these stories, as well as your stories … things just seem to work out! None of the stories in this book have appeared in any other volumes.

I'm pleased that you are reading this book. I would like to meet you personally and get acquainted. When you finish, you will know much more of me than I know of you … contact me, if so moved.

BEN D. MAHAFFEY
Vernal, Utah
bbmahaffey@sbtnet.com

SECTION I – FISHING

•

A few fishing stories from the
Amazon to Alaska
and places in between

My Most Memorable Fish

After a lifetime of fishing; after catching scores of fish around the world … catching a few specific fish always come sweeping back into my conscious memory. And, surprisingly, the details of each experience are still vivid.

The first fish I remember catching is a Brook Trout. However, I may have caught others but this singular fish is the first *memorable fish*. In the 1940's, fishing gear was primitive compared to today's vast array of equipment.

There was a wide selection of flies, but lures were simple; perhaps eight or ten types. As a child, I was in a hardware store and noticed a different spinner. It was silver with a spoon about the size of my thumb nail, a treble hook with a fly tied around it. A new innovation! I paid 15 cents for one and took it home.

My step dad, Dave Mahaffey, had given me an ancient telescoping rod. It was made of steel and one section slipped into the next one until, collapsed, it was about four feet long. Fishing line in those days was mostly made of some type of linen, usually back and fine in texture. A knot was very difficult to remove.

The Brook Trout (*Oncorhynchus mykiss*) was introduced to Wyoming in the 1800's. This was done privately, usually on horseback. No records were kept so it is unknown where the original stocking occurred. The first fish were brought in from Wisconsin, where they naturally occurred.

The fish is one of the easiest to catch but can only exist in the most pure of waters and usually at higher elevations. They exist throughout Wyoming in most of the higher streams and in some lakes. They are small fish, usually 12 inches or less. However, they strike hard, fight hard and are great tasting.

We were fishing a creek called Middle Fork. It was North of Casper, Wyoming, and West of Kaycee. It was a moderate sized creek that could be waded in most places. Few fishermen had boots in those days and waders hadn't been invented. And, as a child, I just flopped around in the creek as I followed Dave as he fished.

I tried the new lure here and there, without success. Suddenly, I noticed Dave ahead of me had just passed through some beaver dams. They were deep as I carefully crossed the top of them. I had neglected to reel in my line and the lure was trailing in the water behind me. I stopped and then started across the more dangerous part of the dam, when, suddenly, behind me I felt a strange tug on the line. I turned and a large Brook Trout had struck the lure and hooked itself without any help from me!

A 12-inch Brook Trout was huge in my eyes. I tried to balance myself on top of the dam as I played the fish. Finally, I reached down and retrieved the fish. This fish, perhaps more than any other, has helped me have a lifetime passion for this great sport.

Fish and Fangs:

Fast forward 50 years to the Zambezi River in Zambia, Africa. I was on a half-day fishing charter for Tiger Fish. We were fishing just above the magnificent Victoria Falls in a modern 20 foot fishing boat. Our guide, a pleasant South African transplant was very competent as he helped land my first fish.

The second largest and the southern-most species of the Tigerfish (*Hydrocymus vittatus*) is commonly found in the Zambezi River and in the two largest lakes along the Zambezi.

Tiger Fish have hard cartilage in the upper part of their mouths causing difficulty in setting the hook. I tried repeatedly to hook one on a Rapalla plug. After a few strikes, the plug's paint was nearly removed by the sharp teeth of the Tiger Fish.

The colors are strikingly bright, orange striped and vivid. The mouth, when closed shows an attractive head. However, when open, the ½" long teeth, both top and bottom, put the fear into any fisherman! The largest one that I caught was, perhaps, three pounds. However, they become huge, often over 50 pounds in the upper part of the river. The world record is reputed to be 236 lbs.

There is an unusual, relatively unknown fish in Northern Australia, called the Barramundi (*Lates calcarifer*). The word Barramundi is a loanword from a Queenslander Australian language of the Rockhampton area, meaning "large scaled river fish." It has other names: Giant Perch, Giant Seaperch and Seabass.

It's found, primarily in the rivers; however, part of its life cycle is in salt water. An unusual fish, when born, all are males. Then, later in life, all turn to females which are bred by younger males, which they once were!

They exist in fresh water rivers. They migrate to salt water, spawn and then return to the fresh water. During the wet season in Northern Australia, any drainage that looks like a river runs wildly from the constant rains. The Barramundi move up these rivers and often get trapped in large holes or where there are spring fed portions of the river, even during the dry season. Some rivers are large enough to have water all year and these contain more of the strange fish.

While hunting Asiatic Water Buffalo in 2005, my hunting party stopped for lunch on Flying Fox Creek. I should say it's a creek during the wet season but a dry stream bed at other times. We stopped at a long spring-fed hole. While my companions ate lunch and rested, I grabbed an ancient rod, rusty plug and tried my luck.

I cast the plug over near a log on the other side of the hole … and to my amazement, a huge, 30 pound Barramundi struck the plug with a passion. The fish was so large that it took four of us to land it over a tall bank in the river … two guys held me as I leaned over the crocodile infested water and my guide slipped into the water and brought it safely out.

Our hunting party ate that fish for days. Although excellent tasting, with white, flaky meat, I was pleased when I saw beef on the menu!

Succulent Salmon:

There are five species of Salmon in Alaska. I've been privileged to catch all five on various occasions. They are: Chinook (King); Coho (Silver); Sockeye (Red); Chum (Dog); and Pink (Humpies). The salmon are generally referred to by their common names.

All of the salmon die after entering fresh water and spawning. The sizes of the fish vary by watershed and all return to that river or creek where they were born. Then they spend their adult life in salt water and return to start the cycle again.

The King is, perhaps, the most treasured trophy salmon, often reaching seventy pounds with the world's record over 100 pounds. The largest King that I have caught is a male of forty pounds. He looks down upon me as I write this story.

I was wading up to my waist in the Aarolic River when he struck my lure on the far side of the river. It took thirty minutes of wading back and forth and two people to land him since we never used nets. After photos were taken, gently I released the male fish into the water to assist in fertilizing the eggs of the females before giving up his life.

Silvers strike the hardest and respond best to wet flies, although I am not a fly fisherman. Sometimes they are so anxious to strike that they knock other fish out of the way to hit first. I once had a large male Silver strike, hook himself and became so violent that he charged in my direction and completely launched himself out of the water and ended up behind me in the grass.

Dog Salmon have an un-deserved bad reputation. This is based on the history of the Natives using the fish to feed their sled dogs. They are about the size of the Silvers, but not as beautiful in spawning colors. They look as if they were painted with water colors and the colors ran down their side before drying. They fight equally hard as the Silvers. They are good eating, although not recognized as such.

The Reds hit poorly and are not very sporty. Their meat is bright red and is very popular to fishermen. I seldom fish for them since they provide less challenge. In fact, a little secret is … most Reds caught are snagged, not hooked.

The Pinks, called Humpies are the smallest of all the salmon and are the species most used for canning. The meat is pink in color and they run around three pounds. I have watched commercial seiners catch them by the thousands and dump them in the hold of the mother ship.

So, my favorite salmon to catch, by preference are: King, Silver, Chum, Sockeye, Pink. My favorite eating salmon by preference, are: King, Sockeye, Silver, Chum, Pink. The King is the oiliest of the salmon and is least known by the public. They all smoke well.

There are two rivers in Alaska that are permanently muddy: the mighty Yukon and the Kuskokwim. The latter is 900 miles long and is in Southwest Alaska. I was attending a hunting and fishing show several years ago in Salt Lake City, Utah.

An Alaskan Native woman convinced me to come to her lodge and fish for a week. Her lodge was in a small village called Aniak. Upon arriving, I was surprised that the river was muddy. In fact, I was distressed, not knowing about the river.

She laughed and told me that we would be fishing in the tributaries and not to worry about the river. We had several days of fishing for Rainbows, Silvers and Grayling on ultra-light tackle.

One day we were fishing at the mouth of a large river spilling into the Kuskokwim. It was so large that the fresh, clear water was not diluted for about a mile downstream. I waded into the clear part and began to catch a few Silver Salmon.

I cast my Mepps spinner up river and began to retrieve it. The lure settled to the bottom of the river and I thought that I was snagged. Suddenly there was a violent shake and the lure started to move across the river!

I knew that I had a large fish on and I knew it was not a Silver. I finally turned the fish back towards me in the swiftly moving river. My guide yelled: "Mahaffey, you've caught a huge Sheefish."

I had heard of the Sheefish (*Stendous leucichthus nelma*), but I had no idea that I would catch one and my plans for the trip didn't include fishing for them.

The fish fought hard in the current but soon became tired and my guide successfully netted it for me. It was about 18 pounds. The fish is found only in the sub-arctic of North America and Asia. In Alaska it if found only in the Yukon and Kuskokwim drainages.

The rest of the morning was spent catching both Silvers and Sheefish, at about the same rate. It's a magnificent fish and one that I will always remember. Most of the fish averaged 18 pounds but they reach a size of 60 pounds. I don't know what I would have done, had I hooked one that large.

The pride of the Amazon

The most beautiful and challenging fish that I have caught is the Peacock Bass, found in several river systems in South America. It has been introduced into some waters in Florida but is not flourishing as those in their native waters.

The fish is not a Bass, but is a Cichla (*Cichla intermedia*) However, it looks like a bass. I suspect it was called bass to begin with to attract the vast number of American bass fishermen to South America.

The Barred Peacock Bass is one of the most exciting fish in the world to catch. This 17 lb. giant was caught on the Unini River, Brazil.

New species are being identified and the exact number has not been agreed upon at this time. Some species are rare and only found in isolated rivers in South America.

The three species that I am familiar with are: the Barred, Butterfly and the Speckled. I have had the privilege of catching all three species in a single day on the Unini River, a tributary of the Amazon River near Manaus, Brazil.

The violent behavior and the awesome tackle-busting power of these fish is what attracted me to Brazil. The Barred species protect their young and will violently attack anything thought to be a threat to the "pods" in which their young congregate on the surface of the water.

Thousands of young fry congregate in the pod, which is like a flat bubble on the water. The pod moves very rapidly around the lagoons, with mom and dad below the surface guarding the movement.

I placed a surface lure near a pod one morning and had an incredible strike. I hooked the fish, of unknown size, and fought if for a few minutes until it broke loose. These fish are considered the most powerful fresh water fish in the world.

The world record size of the Barred is 27 pounds. The largest I have caught is 17 pounds. However, my fishing companion caught a 22, 20 and 18 pounder in an hour one morning.

A Fish by Any Name:

John Hanna, one of my life time friends moved to Idaho in 2005. We were visiting on the phone one day and I asked him if he wanted to float a river and fish for Steelhead. I told him I would bring my boat but then we both agreed we should hire a guide to see how the professional guides catch this prized trophy.

John scheduled a fishing trip with a local guide and John, his wife Nancy and I agreed to meet and fish for two days on the Salmon River. This river is one of the more popular rivers for Steelhead. However, fishing pressure was high and success per fisherman was less than on other rivers.

The Rainbow Trout (*Oncorhynchus mykiss*) is a species of salmonid native to tributaries of the Pacific Ocean and North America and large portions of the

United States. It is a popular species and is favored by millions of fishermen. There are many varieties, based on the hatchery from which they come.

However, the ocean going (*anadromous*) form, including those that return for spawning are called Steelhead. The fish in the Salmon River have 750 miles to navigate if they return from the ocean to spawn.

The first day was enjoyable. John and Nancy had one guide and drift boat and I had a guide and drift boat to myself. The first day we caught several species of trout to keep us interested, but our prime goal was to catch Steelhead. John caught two and Nancy caught one. I was unsuccessful. I didn't even have a strike from a Steelhead.

The weather was magnificent. Wildlife was abundant as we floated away from civilization in several places. I photographed two huge Big Horn Rams from a few yards. My guide began to push me hard to catch a Steelhead and was relentless in his directions.

John and Nancy were successful but I thought that I would fish for two days and not catch a single Steelhead. However, late on the last day, we approached some mild rapids. I intended to retrieve my lure, which was a modified Daredevil, from the swift water. But the rapids grabbed my lure and pulled it down stream! I slowly began to retrieve it when I felt a vicious strike and I knew it was a Steelhead.

The guide pulled the boat into an island as I stood up to better handle the fish. Suddenly the line went limp. I thought I had lost him, however, I soon realized the fish had turned and was facing upstream, letting the force of the water give him a rest.

I decided to get out of the boat to better fight the fish. The guide yelled at me: "stay in the boat, Mahaffey, or you'll lose the fish." I thought about it for a minute and then hopped over the side and moved downstream.

The fish turned, caught the rapids and was gone downstream. However, now, I could chase him. Had I stayed in the boat I would have lost him. We soon had him cornered in a pool. I played him until I could slowly retrieve him into the waiting net.

What a wonderful end to two days of intense fishing for one trophy Steelhead. So, I have çaught one Steelhead in my life! He is mounted on the wall behind me. This was the last time I saw John or Nancy. He died the next spring in Southern Utah, touring the National Parks. I miss him. Nancy has since re-married.

Keep It on the Bottom:

My home in Vernal, Utah is an hour's drive from Flaming Gorge National Recreation area. This is a 90 mile long reservoir which extends from Wyoming into Utah. It is the home of one of the most favorable fisheries in the world for the Lake Trout.

My latest memorable fish is the Lake Trout (*Salvelinus namaycush*). The fish is actually a Char and is often called Mackinaw. Fishermen are attracted to Flaming Gorge from all over the world because of the large fish. The record for the lake is 52 pounds. One day I was in a lodge near the lake where a replica of the fish was displayed. An awesome fish!

Lake Trout are dependent on cold, oxygen-rich waters. During the period of summer stratification, they are often caught in depths of from 60 – 200 feet. They are slow growing and often can reach ages of 25 – 30 years.

Although I often fished at Flaming Gorge, I never fished for the Lake Trout. Most fish are caught on down riggers with a lot of effort and expense. Thus, I was never motivated to fish for them until the spring of 2009.

I have a friend, Del Brady, who suggested that he and I hire a guide and learn how to fish for the large, popular fish. So, we hired one of the local guides for a ½-day trip. I caught one 18-pounder in six hours; my friend nothing. I was not impressed with the way that we fished and soon realized that the guide would only fish one way and was certainly not interested in any suggestions that I might make.

An 18 pound fish is a nice fish. So, I showed it to a dedicated fisherman friend, named Craig Monsen. Craig is a Lake Trout aficionado, especially large ones. He's caught them up to 40 pounds. I know how successful he is because he has them mounted all over his garage. Craig looked at the fish, acknowledged it but didn't say anything.

A week later, he called me and said that he was going up on the "Gorge" on Saturday and would I like to go with him. Several years before, I asked him to take me. He said, "perhaps, some time." And now that some time had arrived.

I had more faith in him than reasonable, but I knew if I could ever catch a large fish it would probably be with him.

Craig tried for other fish but the Lake Trout was always the first priority. We would use his boat. He suggested that I pull the boat with my pickup; I gladly agreed. He said: "pick me up at 3:30 a.m." Now I like to fish but leaving in the middle of the night sort of tests my resolve, but I agreed.

When we arrived at Antelope Flats; daylight was breaking and so we could easily launch the boat. Although June, I was cold and shivering as I slipped on a jacket. There was no other boat action at the ramp but we could see two professional guide boats in the distance.

Craig told me that in the spring he didn't use down riggers to fish at specific depths. Instead we would use a method called long lining. This is using steel line and letting enough out to actually drag the bottom of the lake. We were to use a six inch plug and remove the belly hooks and only rely on the front treble hook.

Craig knows the lake well, after having fished it for over 20 years. There are certain areas that the fish like more than others; he has memorized these areas by land marks and by his sonar. He soon had the rods out and was letting out steel line and directing me to do the same.

There are three variables that control the depth of a lure: the weight of the line and lure; the length of the line; and the speed of the boat. Craig knows all of these well. Soon we both had out between 350 and 400 feet of line. The plug was on the bottom, at 120 feet and I could feel the strong snap and tug, as the plug hit rocks, plants and the muddy bottom.

"How will know I the difference between hitting something and a strike?" I asked. "You'll soon learn," was all Craig responded. Based on the structure of the lake, long runs of a mile or two are made. Then the boat moves over and a parallel run is made in the opposite direction.

By the second run, I was beginning to tire, from constantly having to resist the strong dragging on the bottom, even with a heavy rod. The theory is that this action agitates the fish and they will strike the plug out of frustration.

We reeled in and began the second run. Craig noted that there were several fish appearing on the sonar; he commented, "there's a big one." A few minutes after going over the fish, I felt a strange movement and it didn't feel like the normal resistance. "I think I have a fish on," I yelled at Craig. He reached over and felt my rod and exclaimed: "fish on," and I began to try to land the largest Trout of my life!

I knew the fish was large but didn't know how large. Craig didn't mention the size either. I began the long retrieve. I could feel the fish shake its head and make runs to each side. I looked at the counter of the reel. I had retrieved 200 feet and had another 190 to go. I stopped to rest. "Do you want me to help you," questioned Craig. "Not on your life," I replied, as I continued to reel the fish in.

With 80 feet to go the fish had moved directly below the boat and I was reeling straight up. I began to feel confident that we would land the fish. "I'll bet he's at least 20 pounds I yelled." Finally, we began to see bubbles as the fish began to adjust for the shallow water.

This 30 lb. Lake Trout was caught on Flaming Gorge, Reservoir,
Utah. The huge female was estimated to be 25 years old.

Craig retrieved a huge net and began to prepare for the landing. When I could finally see the fish, I Yelled: "It's huge," and huge it was; 30 pounds. It was an unusually short, fat female, very dark with beautiful spots.

"She's probably 25 years old," Craig exclaimed. "I don't want to kill her," I responded, "let's get her dimensions and photos and let her go. I'll have a synthetic mount made." She was 31 inches long, but one side of her girth was 12 inches!

We carefully handled her and as soon as possible had her back into the water. However, she had been out of the water too long and had lost her balance. Craig moved her back and forth, pushing water through her gills. After what seemed ages, strength came into her tail and she righted herself, swam out 30 feet and descended back into the depths like a giant submarine. "Hey, someone else might catch her again," I yelled as I watched her disappear.

Speaking of "keeping it on the bottom," a recent foray to Alaska resulted in the catching of a very unusual fish. I was fishing on the bottom of 200 feet of water for Halibut but I hooked and landed a Yelloweye Rockfish. The fish is also known as "Red Snapper," and is a delicacy for fish lovers.

They are very slow growing and my fish was estimated to be 90 years old. The larger ones live to be from 114-120 years old. The older they get the more bright their color. Mine was as colorful as if it had been painted "international orange." Because of the slow growing and ease of catching by commercial fishermen, the fish has been depleted in certain locations. They are found from Baja California to Prince William Sound, Alaska. The fish is currently under consideration to be considered threatened or endangered by the government. Unfortunately, because of the depth of water in which they live, they die when brought to the surface. I would have been pleased to release it; instead, I ate it! A synthetic reproduction now graces my wall.

"I fish, therefore, I am." Fishing brings out the poet, the philosopher and the battlefield strategist. Many fishermen have the souls of a naturalist. Could it be that fishermen can relate the whole experience as a metaphor for their everyday lives?

The Chemistry on a Fishing Trip

Never Fish with Women

I don't like to fish with women. This feeling was reinforced the other day while I waited in the office of my favorite Chiropractor. The office secretary and the insurance clerk were talking about going fishing. That doesn't mean that I don't like to do other things with women but not fishing. I wouldn't even want to fish with either of those women, and both were attractive enough to cause me to forget the bait box.

As soon as a woman joins a fishing group or sets foot on a boat, something changes; the chemistry dissolves between the men. Why a guy can't belch, or let any air from any orifice of his body without feeling guilty. Now, I don't have any problem with others fishing with women. Some men are completely compatible with women and I accept that fact.

It takes a total of two or three men to really be fishing buddies. My favorite buddy is also my urologist. This has some advantages at times. But once Dr. Roger Bladderburst sets foot on my boat he's just plain Roger. I don't have to say: "Dr. Bladderburst, would you please hand me a night crawler?" I just yell out: "Buggarhead, throw me the worm box." But, on the other hand, when I have a bladder problem, I can get an instant appointment and not have to answer all of the silly questions that his staff asks me.

Roger and I both have tendencies to become depressed. Both of us have a lot of good reasons to be depressed. When either of us reaches the breaking point, we call the other up and plan a fishing trip. This is usually on Fridays when Roger is not practicing his trade on the innocent. When he wants to go fishing he calls me. But when I want to go fishing I usually go down to his office, which is handy to every place in Vernal. This personal visit is caused by a constant difficulty getting through to him on any phone at home. It appears the problem is centered on a teen-aged daughter and her friends.

One day I was in his office trying to convince him that a fishing trip could keep me from becoming out of control and killing an insurance agent or planting a bomb in the regional IRS office. We had been having great luck on the local reservoirs and we were trying to figure out which one to visit on Friday. Suddenly, from around the corner, a woman emerged and said: "I'll go fishing with you. I love to fish."

It was Bertha Knockworst, Roger's Mother-in-law. I had met her one other time in the office. She was one of his office clerks. She was a little intimidating to me, especially, wanting to go fishing! She also could be physically intimidating. She was a little hefty, about 240 pounds hefty. "I don't like to fish with women," I blurted out before I could think of a more clever lie. "Well, that is certainly a sexist attitude if I ever heard one," she promptly replied and returned to the other room.

Well, that settled that. Roger turned a little red in the face. Roger does that at times. He and I are different in our responses to the feelings of others. He's a gentleman. We continued with our plans. It would be Calder Reservoir on Friday. Everyone was catching them at Calder Reservoir. Indeed we fished two days straight; Friday and Saturday. Now, fishing really has to be good to get Roger out two days in a row. We caught about 60 and released them on Friday but only about 40 on Saturday. We did notice on Saturday that some of the Rainbow Trout appeared to have sore lips.

I never thought much more about Big Bertha, which I began to call her, but not in her presence, of course. The fish had quit biting at Calder Reservoir but were hitting pretty well at Red Fleet Reservoir. Now Redfleet is my favorite Reservoir. I don't like to call reservoirs lakes because lakes are natural and reservoirs are made by man. But if there ever should have been a natural lake, it is Redfleet. It's named Redfleet after the huge, mountainous red sandstone formations that surround the body of water. They look like a fleet of huge ships, mostly battleships. I like to compare Redfleet to Lake Powell, which is actually a reservoir, but no one but me seems to worry about the difference.

When the fish are *not* biting on any of the local reservoirs or lakes, I go to Redfleet. I would rather *not* catch fish at Redfleet than any other place. But they *were* biting at Redfleet and I wanted to get some of 'em! It was early afternoon. I coasted into the parking lot outside of Dr. Bladderburst's office. I sauntered in and said: "Is the sawbones available for a personal consultation." "I think he's asleep in his office," his secretary responded.

I walked back and knocked on the door. Roger answered and we immediately began to plan our Friday's trip to Redfleet. We were about finished and we were arguing about whether to bring sandwiches or finger food, when Big Bertha stuck her head in the door and said: "Ben, please take me fishing with you. I love to fish." "I don't like to fish with women," I politely told her. "Didn't we have this conversation a couple of weeks ago?" I continued. "You are not serious about your feelings towards women are you?" Big Bertha coyly countered.

Now, Big Bertha took me by surprise when she asked me if I was serious about my attitude towards women. Suddenly, I began to think what others in the office might think about me, hearing this loud dialogue. The nurse, the secretary, the receptionist and two patients in the office were all eyeing me with some kind of curiosity, anxiously awaiting my response.

I began to feel a little flushed and embarrassed. "Well, I might reconsider," I answered. "Do you have your own fishing equipment?" "I have everything that I'll need," she responded, becoming so excited that her whole body began to shake with some kind of anticipation, hopefully for fishing.

We continued with our plans, only now two fishing buddies had become three people going fishing. There is a lot of difference between two fishing buddies and three people on a boat together. I began to immediately suppress any thought of an uncontrolled belch. We needed more sandwiches, more worms, and more patience. And besides, now we would have to fish seriously instead of for pleasure. I've had women out-fish me before and it's not a pleasant experience.

Six-thirty is our usual departing time. We can leave home and be fishing at Redfleet Reservoir in exactly 28 minutes, timed and executed. That is a great advantage of living in Vernal, Utah. Roger and Big Bertha arrived on time. I had everything packed and the boat ready to go. Roger brought the food and all of his own gear. I looked at Big Bertha's gear. She had a spinning rod and one lure!!

It is only about ten miles out to Redfleet Reservoir. I have to go through town due north. It doesn't take long; two stop signs and one electric stop light. Sometimes I can slip through all three without notice. This morning was going to be clear, bright and glorious. A celestial day! The sun was barely nipping at the tips of the various colored sandstone formations; gray and brown and then, as we neared Redfleet, a deep maroon color. I noticed on one of the battleship formations that the sun had cast an unusual beam on the two smokestacks, giving them a strangely realistic look. It reminded me of a ship, the USS BOXER, that I had served on over 60 years ago.

There is a campground at the site of the only ramp on the small reservoir. This morning there were three boats in the parking lot, but not a single boat on the water. I made a wide swing and then backed down near the water.

I asked Big Bertha to get in the boat and prepared to launch. I didn't realize that she was quite as heavy until she struggled to lift one very large leg into the boat. Now my boat is not small; it's a 19-foot, deep hulled, Signature Series Lund Tyee, otherwise known as the ultimate fishing boat. It is equipped with a 150 HP Johnson, a 10 HP Johnson trolling motor and a large electric trolling motor with a laser-beam guidance system.

Roger backed the boat into the water until the boat slipped from the trailer. Big Bertha got excited and began to move about the boat. As she moved starboard, it listed starboard, when she moved to port, it listed to port. It's strange but boats do that when large bodies of weight are shifting here and there. I finally got Big Bertha settled down into one of the seats as I cranked up the main engine to make the short run to where Roger and I decided that we would start fishing.

Our secret intelligence sources had informed us that the fish were biting well on large spinners called cowbells and a few other lures. Jigs were successful but I was not going to be in a boat with Big Bertha casting around large jigs in my presence. We decided that the safest method would be to troll. I shut off the large motor and cranked up the trolling motor. It started easily with that sweet, trolling idle sound that only a 4-stroke motor can make.

Roger can get his lure in the water about as fast as anyone that I know. I had to handle all of the other guiding chores, so I was last to begin to fish. Roger immediately exclaimed: "I had a hit, oh, it's hitting again, oh, it's on; stop the motor!" I only had about ten feet of line out and I reeled it in. I was delighted that Roger ad caught the first fish. "We'll show her," I thought. "We'll catch so many fish that she will feel so bad; she'll never ask to go again." I grabbed the net and dipped the fish up. It was a nice Rainbow, about a pound and a half.

Now, Big Bertha watched the whole action with disinterest. She soon had her strange looking lure back in the water. The lure was small, in relation to our large cowbells and it bobbed and wobbled in a lop-sided fashion. I couldn't imagine any self-respecting Rainbow Trout giving it a second look. We moved around one of my favorite rock formations. I was just letting my line out when Big Bertha said: "I have a nice one hooked, would you mind putting the motor in neutral until I land it?" "How do you know how nice it is, until we land it?" I asked her. "I can just tell about fish when I hook 'em," she responded. I handed Roger the net and he quickly landed the fish. It was a beauty, about three pounds. That's about as big as they get in Redfleet.

We continued down the long narrow, red rock canyon. I was just beginning to let my line out again, when Big Bertha quipped: "Oh, I have another nice one on. Would you please stop the boat and help me land it?" I quickly reeled my line in and handed the net to Roger. The fish was fighting a lot harder than the first one. Big Bertha moved from side to side, the boat rocking as she tried to keep the fish from getting tangled in the idling motor. Roger made a last lunge and landed the fish. It was bigger than the first one; three and a half pounds!

Big Bertha's antics had turned the boat around, so I shifted the motor in gear and started West down the canyon. Big Bertha had decided to sit on the rear of the boat, right on top of the rear live-well, with her feet firmly planted on the transom. The only time she moved the rest of the day was to open the cooler for food or to put one of her large fish into the live-well. We had decided early that we would keep the fish. Big Bertha wanted to cook them for her family.

"Bertha, would you mind letting me look at that lure?" I asked her. She politely turned around and placed the strange looking critter into my hand. I memorized its shape and color. She turned back. I frantically searched every drawer of my very large tackle box. I had nothing that remotely resembled the strange apparatus. I would have to use my old tried and true cowbell with a night crawler on the back.

I had about a hundred feet of line out and was seriously fishing when Big Bertha's usual request came: "I have a nice one on, would you mind ...?" As soon as Roger landed the last fish, which was a twin or a triplet of the others in the live-well, I said: "Bertha, would you like to have a sandwich? I pushed the food cooler over where she could reach it. I was hoping that she would quit fishing long enough for me to at least get my line into the water. Big Bertha didn't miss a beat. She had a sandwich in one fat hand and could let out line and fish with the other at the same time. In fact for the next several passes up and down the canyon, fish disappeared from the water and sandwiches disappeared from the cooler. Bertha Knockworst could eat as well as she could fish!

I couldn't figure out why Roger wasn't saying much to me. In fact, he would hardly look me in the eye. Did he know something that I didn't know? He did manage to have two more hits and hooked another fish but couldn't land it. But Big Bertha didn't stop. I began to notice blood and other fish remnants appear all over the back of the boat. Why that woman had spread more gore in two hours than had been deposited on that boat since I owned it. I was embarrassed. I had not had a bite. Roger had one small fish and a couple of bites. It was now 11:00 o'clock and my day was already ruined.

"Have we caught enough fish for you to feed your family?" I asked Big Bertha. "I have nine and they are large so that's plenty," she responded. "Well, let's go home," I suggested. "Oh, not yet, let's make one more pass down the canyon. I'll release any more that I catch. "One more pass. Roger and I will have a sandwich before we go back," I answered. I put my hand into the cooler. All I found was empty sandwich wrappers and one half sandwich. I handed it to Roger and acted as if everything was fine. "How did I get into this situation," I asked myself. It was all Roger's fault. She was his Mother-in-law.

After one more pass and three more large released fish, I cranked up the large motor and headed back to the dock. It was now high noon. A day of fishing ecstasy had turned out to be a day of agony. I let Roger off to retrieve the truck and trailer. I looked into the live-well. Nine huge Rainbows and one smaller one that Roger caught. I was surprised that Roger's fish had not been eaten by the others.

The boat was loaded, all gear safe and secure. I was about to drive away, when Big Bertha said: "Ben, did you bring your camera?" "Yes, it's in the boat," I responded. "Would you mind taking some photos of me before *you* clean the fish?" Roger and I lined up the large fish for several photos. We then cleaned the fish as Big Bertha watched us from the comfort of the truck.

There wasn't much conversation on the way home. I spent most of the time planning what I was going to tell Dr. Roger Bladderburst about what I thought of Bertha Knockworst. I DON'T LIKE TO FISH WITH WOMEN!

What Drives a Man to Fish?

Of Fish and Men

After a lifetime of fishing, I still cannot explain the strange attraction of the popular sport. Others have tried. Henry David Thoreau said: "Many men go fishing all of their lives without knowing it is not fish they are after." President Herbert Hoover, one of the poorer presidents, commented: "Fishing is a discipline in the equality of men; for all men are equal before fish." At least, he had that right.

And so, recently, five of us joined together for a fishing trip to Alaska. Some of us were strangers; some of us had hunted together. Del Brady, the organizer of the group had made similar trips for 22 years, mostly with the same men. Time and age had caught up with all but Brady. So, now a completely different group was organized.

Del's brother Bob and Bob's son Casey, a recently returned missionary, made three. Randy Dearth and I completed the quintet. Bob and Casey were from South Jordan, Utah; the rest of us were from Vernal, Utah

We all met at the airport at Salt Lake City for our five hour journey to Anchorage, Alaska. Upon arrival, we rented a large motor home for our activities on the Kenai Peninsula. Spending ten days with some strangers in a motor home presented some anxiety; but those feelings soon left as I realized how kind and considerate all were to me, the senior participant.

Although the trip was loosely organized, we had an appointment the next day in Seward, Alaska, for a Halibut and Salmon charter. Seward is named after William Henry Seward, President Lincoln's Secretary of State. He instigated the purchase of Alaska in 1867, from Russia, for $7,200,000. This was called "Seward's Folly." The cost was about 2 cents an acre. The one state is 1/5 the land mass of the other 49 states. We need leaders today with such vision!

After checking in with Captain Paul, our boat captain, we learned that a large storm was due the next morning and fishing was in doubt. But we were at the dock at 6:00 a.m. the next morning. The weather report was so bad that Captain Paul told us, if we fish, it will have to be within the protection of surrounding land, and be for ½ day.

This was a poor choice and I suspect that Captain Paul knew that we had little chance to catch Halibut so close. However, we all departed with high spirits. The constant heavy rain and large swells didn't dampen our enthusiasm. We were soon anchored and catching common Cod and Black Rockfish (*Sebastes melanops*).

The evening before, I was feeling ill and now, I had my first experience in being seasick. I spent my full enlistment in the Navy without the scourge but now I know what it's like. Bob joined me in the experience. Neither of us let it stop us from fishing. I call that dedication!

I was fortunate in catching a 28 inch Yelloweye Rockfish (*Sebastes ruberrimus*), reputed to be 90 years old, by Captain Paul. I didn't know much about the fish but I soon learned some astounding facts. The fish is also known as "red snapper" and is a favorite of fish lovers. The fish can live to be 114-120 years old. Because of their slow growing and ease of catching by commercial fishermen, it has been heavily fished in certain locations. It is currently under consideration for listing under Threatened or Endangered status.

The fish become brighter orange as they age and grow to be about 36 inches maximum. I plan to eat it soon and have ordered a synthetic mount to always remind me of the fun I had catching it. How will a 90-year-old fish taste? Some of our group was disappointed in not catching Halibut but we caught many other fish. A fish is a fish!

After collecting our 60 pounds of fillets, we departed that afternoon for Anchor Point, where we would fish for Silver Salmon in the Anchor River. Del had successfully fished this river for years and wanted to return. We toured the river in the evening and planned to fish the next morning.

The author, with his first Yellow-eye Rockfish. The
28-inch fish was estimated to be 90 years old.

The five of us, with full rain gear, silently trudged the half mile to the river in the dark. We were hopeful of getting to the river before all of the resident fishermen. Del wanted us all to try some new lighted bobbers so that we could watch our lines connected to fish eggs in the dark. On my first cast I missed the whole river and got a serious snag on the other side. I have a hard enough time casting when it's light!

We could see the bobbers but the fish must not have seen the eggs because we didn't get a bite. The anchor River is the river of choice for locals and others from all over the world. There are so many fishermen in the short distance legal to fish that the term "combat fishing" aptly applied. At least, I had never been in such a situation before. There were fishermen running up and down the river like the front four of the Dallas Cowboys.

The five of us fished for two days. I caught one very large Pink Salmon. Del caught a 30-inch Steelhead and released it since it's a no-no to keep them. They look so similar to a Silver that you have to look in the mouth to tell the difference. I suspect there is a lot of Steelhead eaten for Salmon! Del and

Randy caught four Silvers during the two days. Bob, Casey and I didn't catch any Silvers.

There were fishermen from all over the world fishing. There were also many local residents. As luck would have it, I introduced myself to a lodge owner named Brian Emard who was guiding some visitors from his lodge.

I could see that he was using bait and caught two Salmon right next to me. Brian showed me how to attach Salmon eggs for bait and gave me the rest of his eggs. Suddenly he looked at me and asked: "How would you like to go to Lake Clark National Park and fish for Salmon on Silver Salmon Creek?"

I was embarrassed not knowing where that National Park was … especially since I taught park management for 20 years. He then told me he takes his clients over by boat for the day. "I'm really interested and I'll call you," I responded.

That evening, I made the suggestion that we all go across the bay and fish and see the National Park. I told them I knew nothing about Lake Clark National Park, but that I could find out information in a hurry.

I soon learned that the Park was established by the Alaska National Interest Lands Conservation Act in 1980, under President Jimmy Carter's administration. The Park includes many streams and lakes vital to the Bristol Bay Salmon fishery. The park includes the junction of three mountain ranges and two active volcanoes (Iliamma and Redoubt).

Redoubt erupted a few years ago and caused days of ash and smoke deposited on Anchorage and other areas. We could see where the southwest part of the volcano had been blown away; steam was coming from a vent. Iliamma was also showing steam from a vent. Originally a National Monument, Lake Clark's status was changed to National park. Two-thirds of the park was designated Wilderness. This National Park is the most remote and least visited in all the system.

None of our party appeared to be interested in making the trip except Casey. The rest wanted to stay and fish the Anchor River. After learning that the fish count at the weir was as little as 17 fish a day, I became even more interested in going. I knew that I had a better chance at winning the lottery than catching any fish on that river. Salmon fishing is easy … if the fish are present. I asked them if they minded if Casey and I broke with the group and made the trip. None objected and all seemed pleased for us.

I called Brian and he told me he had openings for two people on Monday. That would work out well. On Saturday, we found our way to the local Chapel of the Church of Jesus Christ of Latter-Day Saints in Homer. We camped that night in the Chapel parking lot I was confident that the Bishop would be pleased to have five more people join their meeting no matter where they parked. All were kind and accommodating to us. I met the brother of one of my best friends "way up north in Alaska."

Del taxied Casey and me to the lodge at 5:30 a.m. the next day and then left us to go back to the Anchor River. Two older men from Minnesota joined us on the boat. Along the coast of the Cook Inlet, in several places, residents launch large boats directly on the beach. This is accomplished by using huge tractors with over-sized tires to back into the surf. Launchings can be made in high or low tides.

As dawn came, we were well on our hour and one half hour journey to Lake Clark National Park. The volcano loomed larger and larger as we approached the range of mountains. However, there was a smaller range between the coast and the volcano so it became obscured to us. Before we lost sight, the huge mountain loomed above us and we were rendered as insignificant as an ant to a skyscraper.

As we neared the beach a heavy bank of fog engulfed us. I asked Brian if he could find the dock. He laughed at me. There was no dock and the only way to visit was by float plane or wheel plane which landed on the beach during low tide. We would have to anchor out and plan our return, based on the incoming tide!

When the park was formed there were a few isolated private in holdings. One was located a short distance from our landing. As we approached the beach by the private lodge, several people were viewing three bears on the beach. This was not a good omen for fishing!

The landing on the outgoing tide was not difficult, although we did have to wade and carry all of our equipment. A National Park Service employee met us and guided us to the only structure; a small cabin with an electric fence around it. We were briefed on how to behave around the bears. We were also given a large metal container on a cart where we were to put the fish to protect them from the bears. Suddenly, I could feel a bear slapping me around and stealing my fish!

The five of us proceeded across a meadow, across the main river and over to Silver Salmon Creek. This was a beautiful creek, with deep, winding holes. The four of us spread out on the creek. Casey caught the first fish and from then on we all caught, hooked and lost fish for the next two hours. I caught a large Silver and then had two break water and snap my line! I apparently had the drag set too tight.

But … between fish we were chased out of our holes by the marauding bears up and down the creek. If anyone sighted a bear he would yell out "Bear!" We would then retreat, together, back into the brush and wait for the bear to do whatever business he wanted.

Casey was fishing next to me as I watched him hook a huge Silver. Then someone yelled: "Bear!" Poor Casey. He didn't know whether to wrestle the bear or give up the fish. The bear won, the fish got away and he came over with the rest of us.

We all caught our fish and had the most unusual Silver Salmon fishing experience that I have ever had. We had to hurry to cross the main river since the tide was coming in. We had a pleasant lunch at the cabin and proceeded to take our fish and gear back to the beach.

The tide was now coming in and the boat was a hundred yards out. The waves were increasing in size as Brian inflated a raft and rowed out to retrieve the boat. He then maneuvered the boat close enough for us to attach a line to hold it as we all carefully took our gear out to the boat. Although the water was deep, the boat severely rocking, together, we pulled off this difficult and dangerous operation. I'm not sure I would have gone had I known that there was no dock. This was truly a wilderness fishing experience.

Our trip back was uneventful and the huge tractor pulled us out of the incoming tide. We returned to the lodge where Del and the group were waiting for us. Del and the others were very interested as two men struggled to lift a large cooler with all of our fish out of the boat.

Randy asked: "How'd you do?" "We caught all of our fish and had a great time," I retorted. "How was the fishing on the river," I asked. "Never had a bite," he said. By this time Del came up and told me that he had booked another charter boat to fish for Salmon the next day. Even though we had a second charter scheduled in two days, I was pleased not to have to spend a fruitless day fishing on the river.

We drove back to Homer, deposited our fish at the processing plant and spent the night in an RV park. The next morning, promptly at 6:30, we arrived at the dock where Captain Chuck would be our new charter captain. Each charter boat has one deck hand that does most of the work. These men work as hard as they can to assist each fisherman.

Captain Chuck was 68 years old and looked it. We cast off our line and started out for our 1½ hour journey to what we hoped would be a honey hole. We began trolling for Salmon, using downriggers. These devises are designed to keep the lure at a specific depth, hoping to find the fish. Four downriggers were used with different lures and at different depths.

Captain Chuck began barking out orders and yelling and criticizing each of us for not doing *whatever* correctly. We lost two or three fish as we began and then the old Captain really got agitated. He soon settled down and stopped screaming at us. We caught two Silver Salmon and then they stopped biting.

It looked to me as if we might be in a slack tide and we could fish for Halibut. We all disagreed on whether to fish for Halibut *now,* and then continue on for Salmon later on. This would be the only opportunity during the day to fish for Halibut. Captain Chuck finally settled the argument by anchoring and we began to fish for Halibut.

They were biting constantly and within an hour or so, we had our limit of 10 smaller Halibut. We pulled up anchor and then again trolled for Salmon. Within a couple of hours, we caught three large King Salmon. These are the finest of all of the Salmon species and we were all pleased to land three Kings. Although some in the group didn't want to quit fishing for Salmon and fish for Halibut, they soon forgave me for making such a suggestion. Moral of the story: Be flexible and always look for new opportunities. I didn't catch any Salmon but I did catch my Halibut and helped the others with their Halibut.

Casey Brady was delighted to catch his first King Salmon, a 25 lb beauty.

We returned to Homer and deposited our fish at the processing plant. Our pounds of fish were adding up and it appeared we would have enough for all of us to share. One nice feature of our group was that I didn't have to cook after spending an exhaustive day on the water. My energy was gone but not my appetite or my interest in fishing again tomorrow!

We started later the next day, 7:00 a.m. We met on the 44' Ashtikan, A larger, more deluxe boat and far more comfortable than the other charter boats. Captain "B" was in command. His real name was Bryan Bondioli, obviously not Irish. We had an initial meeting where the Captain told us a storm was coming and gave us the choice of trying to find a window before the storm, 35 miles out or to play safe, stay closer, and probably catch much smaller Halibut. This charter was for Halibut only. We all opted to gamble on the longer trip.

Just before departing a wimpy looking man came aboard who was obviously not a fisherman. He turned out to be an economist from the National Oceanic and Atmospheric Administration (NOAA). This is a huge government bureaucracy, one division being the National Marine Fisheries Service. He was about as friendly as a cobra.

He said he was taking a survey of Halibut charter boats. I tried to tactfully question him about how he selected the boats and what his objective was. He immediately clammed up. Having performed such research myself, years ago, it appeared to me since he wouldn't or couldn't talk about sampling or other simple research techniques, there must have been other motives ... especially since Captain B was leading the opposition to an issue in which NOAA would be involved.

Captain B was by far the most competent charter guide. While traveling to our fishing site, he told us of a political problem that will ruin the Halibut charter business. We had been hearing of it at all over the commercial businesses in Homer. There is a proposal to reduce the Halibut limit to one fish per day. This will destroy the charter business. Few fishermen will pay high charter rates for one fish. Captain Chuck, on our other boat, had told us this was his last year in the business, even without the reduction in fish.

The charter business only harvests a small portion of the total Halibut harvested. The policy board is dominated by commercial fishermen. If the limit is reduced, that allocation will be given to the commercial fishermen. This will also be devastating to the local businesses since little of the commercial dollars remain in Homer. Captain B is leading the opposition to this proposal and is hopeful that enough interest can be generated to defeat the unfair and foolish law.

We traveled for two hours to the planned destination. How the Captain could find a honey hole in the entire ocean wilderness is a mystery to me. He knew exactly what he was doing. We were soon fishing in 400' of water with 2 pound jigs, with huge Salmon heads for bait. Bigger bait; bigger Halibut! We immediately began to catch huge, 60 pound Halibut. After learning how to handle the fish, it became a contest between man and the incredible weight and resistance of the fish.

Most of our group landed their fish by themselves, often taking 30 minutes. However, I had to be relieved several times. I just didn't have the strength and energy to continuously fight the fish. Within two hours we had our fish. On slack tide we could use 2 pound weights, but as the tide moved, we had to use much larger weights to keep the bait on the bottom where the fish were located.

*Del Brady, Casey Brady, Bob Brady, Randy Dearth and the
Author with their hard fought, monster Halibut.*

Our deck hand had all of the fish filleted and washed and ready for processing.
The Cold Point processing plant employees met us at the dock and took
our fish. We now had 375 pounds of fillets of Halibut, Silver and King
Salmon, Black Rockfish, Golden Eye Rockfish and Cod. What an incredible
eating awaited us back at home. Perhaps, I have found one obvious answer

to the question "Why do men fish?" Our return trip to Salt Lake City was uneventful, except for one small problem. While dividing up the fish at a parking lot at the airport, the police were called and we had to explain that we were not dividing up marijuana or cocaine! Truth was the Cop didn't know the fish were more valuable than the drugs!

Awesome Action in the Amazon

The small charter plane leveled off at 12,000 feet. "How wide is it?" my companion asked me. "At least 20 miles," I responded. We were talking about the width of the Rio Negro River, where it joins the Amazon River at Manaus, Brazil. I have seen most of the major rivers of the world but this was a sight never to be forgotten.

We were traveling another 250 miles by plane into the heart of the Amazon Basin, one of the last remaining huge rain forest wilderness areas in the world. In a week, I would learn what jungle wilderness is and why they call it "rain forest."

The 10-passenger Caravan suddenly dropped down out of the fog to begin its landing on a rain-soaked dirt runway. The plane, heavily loaded did fine until slowing down and becoming mired in the mud as it stopped. It would take many Natives pushing to enable it to take off later in the day.

We were greeted by Don Cutter, owner and operator of Peacock Bass Trips. com, one of the first American entrepreneurs to establish accommodations modern enough to attract fishermen from around the world. Several natives assisted in unloading our personal gear and taking it to a large passenger boat where we would continue traveling another 70 miles upstream on the Unini River. The Unini River flows into the Rio Negro River. Later I would learn that there was absolutely no human life above us for another 350 miles to the head waters.

Our group of 20 fishermen would divide at the landing strip. Ten would stay there in a modern hotel boat and another group of 10 would travel up river to another hotel boat and spend a week there.

The last 2½ hours of travel were exhausting, caused from a car ride to Salt Lake City, one flight to Dallas, another flight to Miami and an international flight to Manaus and then our charter flight. But the smell, the sounds and the sights of my first experience in the Amazon awakened me to the magnificence of where I suddenly found myself.

The River People

Many natives, living on the river, were employed by the outfitter. I tried to communicate with them, using what Spanish I knew, without success. Brazil was originally a Portuguese Colony and so, over time, Portuguese became the native language. Although there are similarities between Spanish and Portuguese, it didn't help much. I asked the camp manager, who was an Indian, from India, who spoke five languages, how we were going to communicate. He replied: "your guides know enough 'fishing language' to get along." That was barely a true statement.

There are many racial combinations in Brazil, i.e., native Indians and all combinations with Portuguese, Spanish, Caucasians, Blacks. etc. It appeared that the size of the pure Indian strain was small. I began to judge what combinations I saw directly by their height. Most who were serving us were pure Indians. The women were around 4 feet tall and the men were around 5 feet tall.

The women were kind and had compassion in their eyes. Most of the men had a cold indifference in their eyes. The men were fearless, having lived their lives on the river. Some had never been to a town in their lives. All were illiterate. Their only clothing was mostly what fishermen would give them: T-shirts and various discarded fishing clothes. These clothes belied their basic primitiveness.

The men wore thongs or were shoeless, even when in the jungle. They hunted small crocodiles, at night, with their bare hands. They loved to fish and finding a job helping people catch fish was a great opportunity for them. One effective way to make the men smile, was to catch a large fish.

These natives, most of whom had never been to a town, lived their total lives on the river. More fortunate ones had ancient small boats to live on but others had only primitive huts. They raised small gardens, some on top of their boats. Most of their diets came from various fish and animals of the jungle.

Life is tough for these people. Their average life span is a mere 42 years. It is a dangerous place. One guide on the other boat had severe scars on his head and back, caused by an attack by a Jaguar when he was a child. His father killed the cat with a machete. There are three species of Jaguars: one totally black and two different spotted colors. Several of our guides had cuts on their hands and feet. They were delighted to receive band-aids and disinfectant from us.

Life is hard for the river people. The more fortunate live on boats. Some have never been to a city in their lives.

Peacock Bass

The Amazon basin and its surrounding drainage is home to over 3000 freshwater fish species, almost a third of all the freshwater fish species that exist in the entire world. Adventurous anglers will find no harder fighting or more exciting game fish anywhere in the world.

I was drawn to the Amazon to fish, primarily, for the Peacock Bass. Actually, it is not a bass at all. It belongs to the family *Cichlidae*. It was probably called

Peacock Bass to attract the millions of fishermen around the world who love Bass fishing. In our river, there was the Royal Peacock Bass (*Cichla intermedia*) and two sub-species caught. The common names of the smaller Bass were Spotted and Butterfly. I'm not sure of their technical names. Pound for pound, the smaller fish fought harder.

Nothing can compare to the explosive top water strikes, combined with an astonishing ability to break heavy lines, leaders, rods and ruin reels. I had one fish warp the shaft on a new Shimano reel. Several rods were broken by our group. When these large fish hit a lure above or below water, it is called a "blowup," and indeed, that is an accurate description.

After arriving at camp, I heard the rumor that, often, the larger fish cannot be controlled and they will charge into the underwater brush in the water. If they remained hooked, some guides would swim into the brush after them. I learned this first hand by watching my companion hook a 22-lb Peacock which charged into the brush. In a few minutes, our guide "Eddie" took his spring-loaded groper and retrieved the fish. It was the highlight of a week's fishing experiences.

Ed Souders holds his huge 22 lb. Peacock Bass. The world's record is 25 lbs.

Landing a Peacock bass over 10 pounds is difficult. Each fish seems to save one last burst of energy to expend at the boat and often frees itself and escapes. However, when one is landed, it is like winning some kind of a prize. The fish are gloriously colored … bright reds, yellows and browns. The eyes have a florescent maroon ring around the outside that show emotion.

After the first couple of days, at dinner, I noted to the group at my table that the eyes of the Peacock show emotion. "What do you know about fish emotion?" one of my companions replied. "Are you an ichthyologist?" "I know emotion when I see it," I retorted. "Besides, any fish that protects its babies could have emotion in its eyes." Surprisingly, later in the week, most fishermen agreed with my assessment.

One effective way of catching large Peacocks is to find their young. The new fry move about the river in what is called a "fry pod." This is a group of thousands of fry about a half inch long that stay on the top of the water, making a pattern that is easily identified. When a pod is located, a lure can be cast through the pod or near the pod. Unseen from above, are the parents, huge Peacocks. They will attack the lure with intensity difficult to describe. We had two hookups with fish so large that we couldn't hold them and we lost them both.

Other Fish

Occasionally, a Piranha will strike any lure, offering a surprise to the angler. Taking them off the hook is a dangerous job because of their teeth. Their teeth resemble a 10-tooth ripsaw in size and sharpness. They attack with enthusiasm. It wouldn't have surprised me to see them try to chew the prop off the boat! One day we fished for them using meat. They could clean a large piece of meat off the hook before I could tighten the line after casting!

Most of the different fish in the rivers are incredibly colorful. We caught a 35 lb. Red-tail Catfish. It was red on the fins and up its sides. Its body had a mottled yellow-green color, almost like camo clothing. There were several smaller species of Catfish caught. Some of the smaller ones had whiskers 12 inches long.

Perhaps the most interesting fish was one called the *Pirarucu*. The natives usually had their own names for all of the fish. This fish had no common English name. This fish is also called the *Arapaima* or *Paiche*. This fish is the largest, scaled wholly freshwater fish in the world! It can reach 10 feet long and weigh 550 pounds.

To survive reduced levels of oxygen in the water, these fish have physically evolved the ability to simply rise to the surface and gulp air like a Dolphin. This makes it possible to stalk them in a boat and site cast to them. Our group had two hookups but could not hold them. Two fishermen on the lower boat actually caught two of these giant, pre-historic looking fish. I unknowingly had a large one follow my lure to the edge of the boat where it rolled over, in a breath-taking display of arrogance. It took several minutes to regain my composure.

Piranhas are not large but their teeth are. Their two rows of teeth are about the size of a 10-tooth rip saw. Although poor eating, the natives are fond of them.

The Unini River had receded for several weeks before we arrived. However, a few days before we arrived, torrential rains had caused the river to rise four feet. It rained most days we fished and the river continued to rise. The fishing success was diminished as the river rose. However, all of us fished hard and continued to catch a few fish each day. Heavy rain gear was of great value. Now, I know why they call the area a "rain forest."

Food on the Unini

I poked my head into the galley of our boat. "Anna, what is this meat you cooked?" Anna, our hefty Portuguese cook, shook her head indicating she didn't understand my question. I motioned her out to the buffet area and pointed to some meat that looked like pork.

"Oh, Paca, Paca," she replied. I then asked Gary, our Indian camp manager what a Paca was. He disappeared and returned with a photo taken a few nights before of an animal that looked like a cross between a rat and a deer. It had a common meat taste, slightly sweeter than pork.

Our meals were served buffet style and were basically good, although becoming heavy after a week's indulgence. During that time we ate Peacock Bass, Paca, Crocodile (Caiman) tail, Catfish and Piranha. We also indulged in fruits, small, sweet bananas, with thick skins, pineapples, cashew fruit and juice, mangoes, watermelon and honeydew melon. At least that was what I *thought* the fruit was.

Anna was very good at making doughnuts, cakes and other desserts. She was a good-natured woman who also served as a masseuse, earning extra money. For five dollars, stiff, sore fishermen could receive a 30-minute rubdown.

The Fascinating Jungle

The Amazon Basin jungle is a fascinating place. During our total stay, I never saw a single piece of litter of any kind on land or on water. (Exceptions were where nomadic Indians camp each year, seeking Brazil nuts). I never heard a sound of man; never heard or saw the exhaust trails of a single plane.

Large Macaws flew over us regularly, but at great distances. Huge, colorful Parrots were seen but at a distance. This was caused by the great height of the trees, causing the songbirds to be above us in the high canopy. Huge Flickers were seen everywhere and we often heard their loud drumbeat. We saw monkeys, subtlety crossing over us as we hacked our way into hidden lagoons.

The group of natives working at our boat, in various capacities, had an older man, whom they considered their "medicine man." He had greater knowledge of the medicinal value of plants and trees. I asked our camp manager, who communicated well in Portuguese to ask the Medicine Man to take us into the jungle and talk about the various plants and trees.

Both agreed and several other fishermen joined me in taking a half day off from fishing to learn of the plants and trees. We saw so many useful plants that I cannot remember many; however some, like camphor and various laxatives, as well as diarrhea treatments remain with me. Since I had been suffering from the latter problem, I suggested: "cut that tree down and I'll eat it here!"

We saw several species of Bromeliads, as well as Orchids and flowers with unknown names to the natives. The camp manager pointed out a beautiful flower and said: "This is a very valuable plant in Manaus." I looked closely and discovered it to be a common species of Caladium. I raise them in pots, in Vernal, Utah.

Early one morning, Ramon, one of the better guides, suddenly pulled to the side of the river and looked for a small opening in the jungle to seek a hidden lagoon. Soon, he was hacking his way and making a small entrance. The water had risen enough for us to get out and push the boat over a huge log into a beautiful lagoon. Perhaps, we were the only fishermen to ever cast a plug in that water!

The jungle lagoons are as exotic as shown in the movies. They belie the fish and animals hidden beneath the water lilies and other plants.

There were Water Lilies 30 inches in diameter, with large red, pink and white flowers intermittently blooming throughout the lagoon. I quickly noticed that each leaf was protected by inch spines completely surrounding the leaf. The blossoms were also protected by inch spines on the stems. Using fish forceps and pliers, we carefully took several back to the boat to serve as table decorations, much to the delight of the other fishermen.

When entering the jungle, a strange silence seeps over you, broken only by the occasional sounds of birds, or the screeching of monkeys. The jungle is relatively safe during the day, but changes at night when the various animals come alive and begin to look for their prey.

We saw Mahogany trees 12 feet in diameter and 150 feet tall, reminiscent of the giant Redwood trees in California. The Blood tree was interesting. After peeling a section of bark, it bled a bright red sap, used for coloring woven fabric and pots.

The Brazil Nut Tree was amazing to me. Extremely tall, with straight trunks and huge 5 inch seed pods. These pods turn black when ripe and fall to the ground, threatening anything below. The natives take a machete and cut off the top of the pod and the Brazil Nuts are arranged in the pod like the sections of an orange. They gather these nuts in hand woven baskets, placed in primitive boats and taken down river to where larger boats eventually move them to the market in Manaus.

The Pain of Travel

Travel is becoming increasingly painful and expensive. The security measures imposed on travelers in this country and in foreign countries is intimidating, often foolish and unnecessary. In spite of these experiences, once arriving at unique places of the world, I find the efforts mostly worthwhile.

Travel, whether foreign or domestic, is life altering and incredibly educational. The people, the food, the culture, the environment, all become blended into one great experience that cannot be obtained in any other way other than being there, in person.

The problem with visiting these exotic locations is that one often wants to return. In any case, a return trip must be compared to the many, yet unknown places that remain unvisited. Alas, so many fish and so little time …

SECTION II – HISTORY

●

These are general historic accounts
about one of my heroes —
Theodore Roosevelt, as well as some
af my own experiences

"I put myself in the way of things happening ..."

Theodore Roosevelt – The Man

Part I

Roosevelt was a many sided man and every side was like an electric battery. Such versatility, such vitality, such thoroughness, such copiousness, have rarely been united in one man. He was not only a full man; he was also a ready man and an exact man. He could bring all his vast resources of power and knowledge to bear upon a given subject instantly.
—John Burroughs

Theodore Roosevelt is arguably the most fascinating man to ever be President of the United States. He was certainly the most experienced hunter, gun advocate and conservationist. He had more experience in his 60 years than any other five men. Unfortunately, he died young from congenital heart failure. What would he have accomplished had he lived another 20 years?

He lived in a most exciting time in the history of this nation and the world. He was born in 1858. At the age of seven, he and a childhood friend, a girl, who would in the future become his second wife, Edith Carrow, watched Abraham Lincoln's funeral procession from an upstairs window of his grandfather's house on Union Square, New York city. Little did he know that he would, in his own way, be equal to Lincoln, for his contributions to the nation and to the world.

In 1880, he graduated from Harvard, *magna cum laude*, and was a member of Phi Beta Kappa. He went to Columbia Law School for two years, but quit for some unknown reason and never became an attorney. However, that mental training would serve him well the rest of his life.

In 1882, TR published his first book, THE NAVAL WAR OF 1812. This book set the standards of naval strategy at the Naval Academy for many years. He went on to write a total of 39 books. He served in the New York Assembly, which began his political career.

He stated: *"I put myself in the way of things happening; and they happened ... During the three years' service in the Legislature, I worked on a very simple philosophy of government. It was that personal character and initiative are the prime requisites in political and social life."*

TR seriously followed that philosophy the rest of his life. He was always in the way of "things happening" in politics, war, scientific research, hunting and in caring for his family. Perhaps, it would be more accurate to say that he **made things happen.**

TR was not known to be religious as far as participation in any organized church was concerned. However, he respected religion and was dedicated to the role and protection of religion in the public life. He made one statement that, perhaps, summed up his philosophy:

*"I wonder if you recall one verse of Micah that I am very fond of — **'to do justly and to love mercy and to walk humbly with thy God.'** That to me is the essence of religion. To be just with all men, to be merciful to those to whom mercy should be shown, to realize that there are some things that must always remain a mystery to us, and when the time for us to enter the great blackness, to go smiling and unafraid.*

"That is my religion, my faith. To me it sums up all religion, it is all the creed I need. It seems simple and easy, but there is more in that verse than in the involved rituals and confessions of faith of many creeds we know."

Although TR's career started in the New York Legislature, he went on to become New York City Police Commissioner, Governor of New York, National Civil Service Director, Assistant Secretary of the Navy, Vice President and then finally, President. He was elevated to President when William McKinley was assassinated in 1901. In 1904, he was elected President on the Republican ticket.

He was married twice. His first wife, Alice Lee, died after childbirth and he later married is childhood friend, Edith Carow. This was the girl who sat beside him in the upper window as they watched the funeral procession of Abraham Lincoln in 1865. That marriage resulted in the birth of one girl and four boys. The eldest son, Ted, was named after him and then there was Kermit, Archie and Quentin.

His daughter by Edith was named Ethel. Alice was named after her mother. All the children were reared together. There are many humorous stories of the six children living in the White House and their escapades.

Although all the boys were familiar with guns, it was Kermit who became TR's companion on his 11-month Safari in 1909. Although he loved his sons dearly, he expected them to perform well in every aspect of their life. This is impossible, of course, and was reflected in each son's future.

Upon the death of his wife and mother the same day, he traveled west and established two ranches in North Dakota, the Maltese Cross and the Elkhorn. In those days, the vast lands of North Dakota and in other states were public domain. TR simply selected a good place, constructed buildings and corrals and it became a ranch. He never owned any deeded land.

Other ranchers did the same thing. Cattle were turned out on the open range, year round and had to fend for themselves on the natural grass. Roundups were usually conducted with nearby ranchers and then the cattle were divided, according to brand and new calves branded and then turned loose again. Other roundups were conducted to select cattle to be shipped to market.

TR knew nothing about ranching, of course, but he learned fast and was involved in all aspects of the operations until he was satisfied that he could do what others could do, and sometimes better. He had ranch foremen who took care of the operations while he was gone. He was deeply involved at this time in politics and so he traveled back to New York often. In realty, he didn't spend much more than a year total in North Dakota.

At this time he signed a contract to build a house in Oyster Bay, right outside New York City. He called it Sagamore Hill, in honor of Sagamore Mohannis, the Indian chief who used the hill as a meeting place during the 1660s. This home would be his only permanent residence the rest of his life and would play an important location for political activities and was revered by all of his children.

The winter of 1886-87 was the most severe in decades in North Dakota. TR and neighboring ranchers lost most of their cattle, some as many as 80%. TR lost an estimated 60%. This effectively ended his ranching career. He returned to the ranch a couple of times but it was never used again. Since the ranch was on public domain, it soon fell into disrepair. Nothing remains of it today. However, that area and other areas to the north have become three parts of the Theodore Roosevelt National Park.

Although TR's reputation made the whole area famous, especially the town of Medora, the national park was mostly politically created for his memory than for the natural significance. It was a national historic park first and should have remained in that classification. However, the area is in the badlands and it is useful for a portion of them to be preserved forever.

TR loved that part of the country, although, at that time he had not seen much of the other wonders of the west. He stated: *"It was still the Wild West in those days, the Far West of Owen Wister's stories and Frederic Remington's drawings, 'the soldier and the lost Atlantis, gone to the isle of ghosts and strange dead memories …' in that land we led a hardy life. Ours was the glory of work and the joy of living."*

TR authored three hunting books as a result of his time spent at the ranch and in other western hunting expeditions. He also wrote a large volume on his experiences on an eleven month safari to Africa. One of his earlier books was illustrated by the Frederick Remington mentioned above. Many of the famous men of the west, at that time, were known by TR.

TR's favorite guns in his early hunting experiences were the .40-90 Sharps and later the Winchester lever action .45-90. Although, I am sure at times, he tried other calibers. Scopes were not available in those days; buckhorn and peep sights were used.

In certain ways, TR had conflicting codes of hunting that was not practiced by others. He expressed his opinion that he wanted his shot placed behind the shoulders on most game, but because of open sights and long distance shooting, he reported he made shots in every part of the body. At another time he said that he kept shooting "until the game was down, out of sight or out of ammunition." His hunting ethics will be discussed in detail in Part III of these chapters.

Guns fascinated TR and he owned many through the years. During his lifetime, gun technology was evolving, with many new calibers and types of guns available. He preferred the lever action and reports indicate that he seldom shot anything else. His eyesight was poor, in the early days of his hunting. By time he went to Africa, he was blind in one eye!

Conditions for hunting were greatly different during TR's western hunting experiences. He ran game down with horses and with various kinds of dogs. He reported in his books that he hunted wolves, antelope, deer and bears; having dogs kill them when the animals became exhausted. That type of hunting sounds strange and brutal. Apparently, the greater challenge was the horsemanship.

Most of the American Buffalo were destroyed in the west by the time TR arrived. However, he did kill one or two. According to others, he made a very poor shot and the final kill was not pleasant. Actually, TR was not a good shot, according to others. This was caused by his poor eyesight and open sights. I suspect that he would have done much better had he used the modern scopes.

During his ranching time, wildlife was disappearing and TR lamented that fact many times in his writing. He knew the game would soon be totally gone. But, according to his own writing, he certainly assisted in its demise. He fed his men with deer and antelope and reported going after them in wagons to bring more back. Sometimes he would bring singles back and at other times, kill the game and then pick them up later. Elk were still available and he did his share of killing before they disappeared.

According to one hunt report, in Colorado, he willingly killed six elk; on another hunt he killed three grizzlies. In a remote section of the badlands near his ranch, he killed two of the last big horn sheep. The meat was never wasted. In those days meat was the main staple for the cowboy and wild game made up most of the diet.

On one of his last trips to the ranch, he stated that hardly any game remained over the vast area that he had previously hunted. This appeared to distress him and may have been one reason for his losing much of his interest in returning to his ranch area in the badlands.

On his very last big game hunt of his life, on a moose hunt in Canada, he killed two bulls. His license was for only one bull. Apparently the guide had to make up some kind of report that the second animal had to be dispatched for the safety of the ex-President.

The above statements are for domestic hunting in the west, which he loved. However, he hunted in the south on occasion and in the northeast. Although he hunted waterfowl and upland birds, he made few statements about that type of hunting. He shot a Fox side-by-side 12 gauge.

In 1898, the United States was at war with Spain, over the sinking of the ship Maine, in the harbor at Havana, and for other disagreements, including Spain's presence in the Philippine Islands. TR was a strong advocate of the Monroe Doctrine, i.e., no foreign nation would be allowed a foothold in the Americas.

He had been calling for war through articles and his personal contacts. He wanted a commission as colonel, in the regular army, but because of politics, he was refused. In the spring of 1898, with approval from Washington, he formed an all-volunteer regiment of cavalry. This would be one regiment of a cavalry division.

His regiment was made up of selected men, from all over the nation. Most were from the west, made up of ranchers, scouts, cowboys, fur traders and guides. However, some were his acquaintances from Harvard and the Ivy League schools in the east. There were thousands more applicants than those accepted.

According to Roosevelt's book ROUGH RIDERS, he, as a lieutenant colonel, commanded a regiment of 490 men. He was in two battles, a minor one and the one for which he became famous; the storming of San Juan Hill. This was the major entrenched fortification in Cuba.

The handling of the war by the politicians was a combination of incompetence, poor communication and rivalry. Roosevelt, after spending weeks training his men in horsemanship, marksmanship and obedience, embarked from Texas to Tampa, Florida, on a train. Upon departure from Tampa, to Cuba, Roosevelt was told to leave all of the horses in Florida, with the exception of horses for senior officers. This, in effect, made the cavalry foot soldiers. They had no training as infantry and little equipment.

At that time, the army, in general, was poorly equipped. Roosevelt had to compete with the regular army for equipment and supplies. There was no body armor and no helmets. The men wore western hats and had very poor footwear. After the battle, before being shipped home, Roosevelt fed his troops by buying food locally, with his own money.

Rifles, ammunition and other equipment weren't standardized. Although the new, effective Model 1895 Winchester had been developed, the army never adopted it. Instead, old Springfield Trapdoor single shot rifles, using black powder were issued. The two common rifles assigned were the M1888 rifle and the M1873 carbine. They were in the .45-70 caliber. Before modern ammo development, huge calibers were used. Gatling guns were used during the battles, but not under Roosevelt's command.

The senior officers had horses. TR was assigned two; however one drowned when landing on the beach. He rode his other horse for several days in the battles. Incredibly, he led his troops against Spanish soldiers and marines, on the horse, toward fortified positions, up hill, against modern weapons, with smokeless powder, yet neither he nor his horse was injured.

TR doesn't mention any rifle that he used. Of course, on horseback, a carbine would have been best, even in a scabbard. He stated that he killed one Spanish infantryman with his handgun at point blank range. Other than this single instance, he doesn't mention other guns or his personal marksmanship.

As often the case, military statistics are conflicting. The following are Roosevelt's figures. He commanded 490 men, not counting those missing or in the hospital. TR began as deputy commander of the regiment, promoted to Colonel and then commanded the regiment. Of the total cavalry division of 2300 officers and men, 375 were killed and wounded. In the division over one fourth of the officers were killed or wounded. Roosevelt stated that twice the number of officers were killed or wounded and that *"was as it should be."*

In the total battles, the Spanish had 4500 men against 6600 Americans. The American losses were considerably higher, caused by the nature of routing fortified positions. Malaria caused several deaths and scores to become ill. Although not stricken down like most other men, Roosevelt contracted the disease. Later in his life he would suffer many severe attacks. Long delays in decision making at Washington caused increased sickness by delaying returning home. Senior officers were forced to rebel against the Secretary of War before orders to return were given.

TR and others believed that he should receive the Medal of Honor for his valor in the battle of San Juan Hill. Jealousy from regular army officers prevented this. However, on the 100th anniversary of the battle, Roosevelt received the medal posthumously by President Bill Clinton. The rough riders, as they were famously described, became life-long friends to Roosevelt. They admired him, supported him and kept in contact with him the rest of his life.

TR authored four volumes on hunting during his lifetime. Three were about hunting in the western United States. His most detailed, and by far his most interesting is his report on his 11-month safari to Africa. Titled AFRICAN GAME TRAILS, it was published in 1910. It became very popular and is still available today.

Theodore Roosevelt –
The Hunter and Conservationist

Part II

Personally, I feel that the chase of any animal has in it two chief elements of attraction. The first is the chance given to be in the wilderness; to see the sights and hear the sound of wild nature. The second is the demand made by the particular kind of chase upon the qualities of manliness and hardihood ...
—*Theodore Roosevelt*

In March, 1909, Theodore Roosevelt attended the inauguration of the new President, his friend, later to be his enemy, William Howard Taft. Roosevelt had decided not to run for a third term, although he would have certainly been elected again, had he chosen to run. At that time, it was considered appropriate to only serve two terms and TR had impetuously stated that he wouldn't run for a third term. His wife immediately told him that it was a mistake to make such a statement. TR, personally, selected and groomed Taft to follow his philosophies and to continue his policies.

Taft had served under Roosevelt in his Cabinet, but he was weak and ineffective as President. By 1912 they had become bitter enemies. TR had decided that he wanted to be nominated and run for President again. The Republican establishment wouldn't support him and chose Taft again. Most knew that Taft couldn't win another term because of his poor performance, but TR had many enemies in the higher ranks of the party.

TR broke from the Republican Party, formed the Bull Moose Party and ran against Taft and Woodrow Wilson. This split the conservative vote and Wilson, a Democrat was elected. However, TR ran a great campaign and won 83 electoral votes; Taft won none.

In later years, Taft and TR met several times but TR never forgave him. Taft adored TR and would have reconciled. At TR's funeral, Taft was one of the last to leave the cemetery. He stood off, by himself, crying.

TR's plans for an African safari had been in his mind and in the making for years. It was a gigantic endeavor. TR was, unknown to most people today, a prominent ornithologist, taxonomist and historian. Because of his world reputation, he had many advantages for planning such a trip. He received funds and support from the Smithsonian Museum of Natural History and the New York Museum of Natural History. He had scientists and taxidermists accompany him on all legs of the safari.

His entourage was huge, with a reported 100 porters to carry the burdens of the group, which included four tons of salt for preserving specimens. He even had a large number of books to read on the trip, the contents of which he called his "Pigskin Library." This was so named because of the leather protection for the books.

TR had horses and used them extensively while the bulk of the safari had to walk. He had a huge wall tent, with all of the comforts of that day. After setting up the tent, he always had a large American flag directly in front of the entrance.

The various countries that he visited in Africa have mostly been re-named and are now described as some sort of democracies; few are, and most African countries now are in incredible disorder. In those days, some were British Colonies, with others belonging to the Dutch and Germans. All of the English Colonies were aware of the TR safari in their area. All went out of their way to accommodate and assist the safari. Several times he was treated as a foreign dignitary, having to suffer the pomp and circumstance of such a person. His reputation was renowned throughout the world.

Transportation by train was common and trains had been built in wild, dangerous parts of Africa. Between various legs of the safari and in general travel, TR enjoyed the trains. Sometimes he rode on the cow catcher, a protective devise in front of the engine.

Roosevelt was probably the most famous person in the world. Having been President for two terms, author, Nobel Prize winner for ending the Russo-Japanese war and, of course, his contribution in winning the war with Spain. Often at various train stops, crowds awaited the opportunity to see him.

The choice of what firearms to take on such a trip was important and TR spent a lot of time in deciding. Details are not available about the total number of rifles taken on the safari. Several of his staff was hunters as well as scientists. We don't know what rifles they preferred, nor do we know what rifles others who joined the safari on occasion used. However, we do know that after a year of planning, they ended up transporting 15 wooden crates full of rifles, ammunition and spare parts for the expedition.

According to TR's account of his Africa hunt, he used three different calibers – the .450-500 Holland (H&H) side-by-side double, the Winchester .405 lever action and the Army Springfield .30-06. A large group of prominent friends and professionals presented TR with the .450-.500 while he was president. It appears that he didn't know or wasn't interested in the .375 H&H that had just been developed. This gun was superior to the .405.

The 1895 Winchester was designed by John Browning and was the first Winchester to accept the new smokeless high powered rounds that were revolutionizing the shooting world. This was the first lever action with a magazine instead of a tube to hold the large, pointed bullets.

TR had been exposed to the receiving side of the new smokeless powder at San Juan Hill, Cuba when he stormed fixed positions. The Spanish had new Mauser rifles with smokeless powder. These advantages caused more casualties to the Americans than the Americans did to the Spanish with their outdated powder and guns.

The 1895 Winchester lever action .405 made for the perfect gun for medium sized African animals. The smaller animals would be dispatched with the .30 caliber. There are some indications that an 1895 Winchester lever action .30-40 Krag was used by Kermit.

Roosevelt had to have ... not one ... not two ... but three of the .405 Winchesters. We don't know who paid for them all, but I suspect that

Winchester gave him at least one for the publicity of using it on such an ambitious hunting adventure. Roosevelt declared: *"personally, I prefer the Winchester."*

This statement was only partly true or incomplete because he used the .450-500 for the Elephant, Rhino, Cape Buffalo and Hippos. He stated that he usually carried the Springfield and the gun bearers carried both of the other calibers. Of course, when stalking any of the larger animals he would be carrying the double barrel. TR and Kermit also hunted birds, but other than an Ostrich, little is mentioned. For bird hunting TR used a double barrel Fox 12 gauge, which he commented: *"no better gun was ever made."*

In an unusual presidential endorsement, TR wrote in SCRIBNER'S MAGAZINE: *"The Winchester .405 is, at least for me, personally, the medicine gun for lions."* He should know about Lions since he killed nine and Kermit killed eight. At that time, in eastern Africa, in most of the colonies, the Lion was considered "vermin" and as many as possible were eliminated. Hunters killed Lions, Lionesses and Cubs.

The .405 was discontinued in 1932. Teddy had one Lion and one Lioness charge him, in addition to a Cape Buffalo, two Rhinos and a couple of serious Elephant encounters. The .450-500 apparently took care of all of those critters. The recoil was painful and some were to have said that they would rather face the elephant than the recoil. In his accounts of charging animals, he wrote as if it was a normal encounter and of no great consequence.

The .405 caliber is available today. In 2008, a commemorative .405 was made by Winchester in two grades. This was to celebrate Roosevelt as an important conservationist. In 2009 another commemorative was manufactured to commemorate his 1909 safari. These commemoratives are readily available, but rather expensive. The original .405 Winchester lever action can still be purchased. As a matter of fact, I purchased one last week, new-in-box. I hope to use it for hunting in the future.

Using a lever action rifle has been a new experience for me. I was never attracted to that style, simply because everyone around me shot a bolt action. Sighting it in has been an unusual experience. Using open sights is a new challenge, after using a scope for my whole lifetime of hunting.

During a recent visit to the Buffalo Bill Museum in Cody, I was pleasantly surprised to see a display about TR and his .405 Winchester. This was one of the guns that he used in Africa. As I examined it, I noticed he had it customized. He had installed a modest cheek rest and a recoil pad. It showed it had certainly been used around the world. Estimated value – one million dollars!

The African safari was amazing in the size of the entourage and the number of animals killed. Together, TR and Kermit killed 512 animals; TR -296 and Kermit – 216. The other members of the safari killed many animals and collected scores of various specimens, including birds. Many specimens were not identified at the time TR wrote his memoir. There were several new species identified on the expedition.

Most of the animals were minor. This doesn't mean that they were not sporty or insignificant. Often, it's a great accomplishment to kill all species of an animal. TR and Kermit killed several animals classified as "The Big Five." The following statistics are for his major animals:

Lion	9
Elephant	8
Rhinoceros (square-mouthed)	5
Rhinoceros (hook-lipped)	8
Hippopotamus	7
Zebras (2 species)	20
Giraffe	7
Cape Buffalo	6
Eland	5
Oryx	10
Wildebeest	5
Hartebeest (4 species)	33
Waterbuck (2 species)	11
Gazelle (4 species)	28
Birds (large)	21
Crocodile	1
Python	3

It's unclear how many animals were used as specimens and how many were harvested for food for the large number of natives. He said on several occasions that he went out for meat for the natives, who ate little else. It can be assumed that those used for specimens would also be used for meat. There were times when natives from nearby villages took advantage of the opportunity to have the gift of large amounts of meat.

TR went on several hunting expeditions while president, but not to the extent that he did in prior years. While he was ranching, he took several extensive hunts in North Dakota and surrounding states, as mentioned before. His hunting ethics will be discussed in detail in Part III of this series.

Roosevelt was a complex person, as are most accomplished people. After he recovered his health as a youth and for the rest of his life he relished in doing difficult, physical activities. He was a good horseman and exhibited this talent all of his life. He hiked extensively while president in nearby parks. He often forced prominent guests from around the world on his hikes, often to their discomfort. He took his children and their friends hiking and became their friends, to their delight.

While ranching, he insisted on doing everything all of the cowboys did, at least enough to know and understand the rigors of such a life. He often went hunting by himself with nothing but a frying pan, a few groceries and a modest bedroll. He hunted and explored many times by himself and was proud to do so. He went on roundups with neighboring ranchers and cowboys, taking his turn in all of the duties of such a company.

Once, while in a saloon in Montana, he was ridiculed by a drunk over the fact that he was wearing glasses. He promptly knocked the bully out before he left the saloon. TR drank very little, although his political enemies often accused him of being a drunk. He stated that on his safari to Africa, he drank less than a half pint of liquor. This indicated great restraint, realizing the number of life threatening experiences he had while hunting!

While President, he exercised often in various activities, including tennis. He had his special friends, often foreigners and cabinet members. His partners were considered a select group; others felt slighted for not being invited. He was extremely aggressive in all activities.

During his presidency he had professional boxers come to the White House and spar with him. On one occasion, he was severely hit in the eye, to the extent that it blinded him. He seldom mentioned his problem, but from then on, including on his safari and his Amazon expedition, he had but one eye. He was a voracious reader, but using one eye didn't appear to slow him down.

Since he appeared to be a knowledgeable conservationist, I don't understand his life's history of his slaughtering game, knowing full well, that game management was needed … at least for other hunters. However, this criticism does not detract from his political and personal achievements.

He started the Boone and Crockett Club to emphasize sport hunting and the keeping of accurate records for historic purposes. While he was President, he had the authority to set aside national forests without congressional approval. He set aside so many millions of acres that congress removed his authority.

However, he instigated later legislation called the Antiquities Act, which gave Presidential authority to set aside national monuments. He declared Devil's Tower in Wyoming as the first one. Often, he and other presidents would declare national monuments to secure the land and then Congress could change the status to national parks. He also set aside many wildlife refuges for animal and bird protection.

A personal visit with John Muir in Yosemite National Park changed him forever, in desiring to preserve national and world natural treasures. He declared The Grand Canyon a national monument, which was later changed to a national park.

His curiosity, sense of adventure and boredom about killed him on his famous Amazon expedition. He, Kermit and several others, with native crews went in search of the "river of doubt." This river was uncharted. It was apparently known where the river joined other rivers, but the river itself was uncharted. It would later be named Rio Roosevelt.

They charted it as best they could with the crude instruments. But the nature of the valleys, rapids, incredible insects and topography made for several catastrophes. On one occasion, most wooden boats were lost and new canoes had to be fashioned out of logs. Crewmembers were drowned; one killed a fellow member and then disappeared,

TR had severe attacks of malaria, in addition of a severe infection of his right shin bone. Towards the end of the trip, his heart began to fail him. They had no idea, at that time, where they were in reference to the merging of the rivers. Roosevelt became bedfast and couldn't contribute to the expedition.

I have great understanding and sympathy for what they went through. I have floated and fished the Unini and Rio Negro rivers, north of the river they were exploring. However, those rivers were quiet and navigable. We had all of the latest technology and equipment. I spent one day exploring the jungle, to get a feeling of what it is like. The jungle is dark, dense and foreboding; not for the faint hearted.

Finally, TR told Kermit and others to go on and not risk their lives for his sake. He was sincere in his statement. Kermit refused and within a few days they had finally emerged and ended their journey and found others to assist them. TR was so ill he had a difficult time returning to the United States. This experience had a profound physical and psychological effect upon him. It no doubt, contributed to his early demise. TR had stated that he would live to be 60. He was prophetic with that number.

He was the prime instigator of the Panama Canal, working with complex issued in Central America. This is, perhaps the greatest project ever completed by man. A history of this feat shows his remarkable political abilities. Roosevelt felt that the canal was important for national security. The canal would permit the U.S. fleet to move rapidly from ocean to ocean.

He won the Nobel Peace Prize for negotiating the end of the Russo-Japanese War. He stated at the time, that he was concerned about Russia, but that the United States would have to eventually go to war with Japan. Forty years later, his opinion would come true.

Space does not permit a discussion of his eight year history of legislative accomplishments in ending huge trusts and monopolies that were a great burden to the nation. Suffice it to say, they were extensive.

TR wrote 39 books on various topics, scientific, political, history, hunting, naval tactics, etc. The last book that was edited for him, shortly before he died was titled THEODORE ROOSEVELT: LETTERS TO HIS CHILDREN. He stated that of all his books, he was most proud that this one was published.

During TR's presidency he created 51 wildlife reservations; the first federal irrigation projects; national monuments and conservation commissions. He quadrupled America's forest reserves. He created the Wichita Mountain reserve and Montana's National Bison Range.

These latter actions may have been stimulated since he knew that he helped kill the last of the buffalo in the 1880s.

In addition, he established five National Parks and many National Monuments. With his signature as a conservation weapon, he created, for posterity, a legacy of over 234 million acres. This is about 10% of the nation's land mass.

It's probably unwise to compare the talents and characteristics of our Presidents. TR, during his tenure, was more liberal that the Democrats in many ways; more conservative than the Republicans in other ways. He had more scientific talents than Thomas Jefferson.

He authored more books than any President. Although Lincoln saved the Union, Roosevelt saved our natural resources. He was one of two Presidents who was shot and survived. But perhaps more endearing to me was his ambition, self-pride (perhaps too much), and his love of guns and hunting.

The Hunting Experiences
of Theodore Roosevelt

Part III

Volumes have been written about Theodore Roosevelt's (TR) life and activities. Several new volumes by biographers have recently been published. The Theodore Roosevelt Association has been having national meetings discussing his life for 92 years.

Dickinson State University of North Dakota has an annual symposium about his life and has a division of the university called The Theodore Roosevelt Center. In the western portion of North Dakota, there is a Theodore Roosevelt National Park, comprising three units. Since Roosevelt had a Dutch lineage, there is a Roosevelt Research Center in the Netherlands.

I recently attended the above seminar at DSU. On an excursion to the southern North Dakota Badlands, I had the opportunity to view the location where TR shot his one and only Buffalo (Bison). This kill was accomplished after days of difficult hunting in the most inhospitable environment.

Roosevelt wrote four volumes on his hunting experiences and these experiences are referenced in many other of his publications. He was, without question, the greatest hunter and gun expert to ever be president. Other presidents have hunted but never to the extent of TR's experiences.

Critics have described his hunting as a strange "blood lust." These feelings are described by those with little or no understanding of the hunting sport. However, in all of my research, I have never discovered a serious discussion of TR's hunting ethics or lack thereof.

However, others regarded his "blood lust" more in relation to his political policies, especially the glory of war. TR said: *"All the great masterful races have been fighting races. It is wholly impossible to avoid conflicts with the weaker races. The most ultimately righteous of all wars is a war with savages."* Later, surprisingly, he won the Nobel Peace Prize for mediating the Russo-Japanese War. He predicted that the U.S. would **have** to go to war with Japan decades before it happened.

"Blood lust," when referring to hunters, indicates that hunters enjoy the actual shedding of the blood of an animal. This is foolish, of course, because most hunters consider the blood-letting a necessary but climax of the total experience of the hunt. This includes the planning, travel, comradeship, marksmanship and stalking.

What we are discussing is ethics … *"a system or code of morals of a particular person, religion, group, profession, etc."* Most ethics in America emanated from the Judo-Christian religion, social pressures or lack thereof. Standards or ethics have to be based on some higher guidelines. These guidelines may be developed by the group itself or by a higher level of beliefs willingly or imposed upon the participants.

As the higher guidelines, or moral base, for ethics change, so do the ethics. A current example is co-habitation without nuptials. This activity is generally accepted by much of society, although those who accept such activities apparently don't have a higher level of guidelines or morals evolving from their religion. If their religion accepts such actions, then, generally, that religion, over time, must have changed its doctrine.

Modern warfare ethics are supposed to be dictated by the Geneva Convention Rules of War. It appears strange to me that when nations are trying to destroy nations, there should be guidelines! There were no guidelines for the attacks on Pearl Harbor or on the World Trade Center in New York City. The ethics are generally discussed over the treatment of prisoners. However, our enemies have never followed such ethics.

The basic weaknesses of man require the teaching of morals, standards, guidelines … ethics. The basic nature of man indicates that without these teachings, most behavior will become self fulfilling. We are seeing the degradation of ethics as our society becomes increasingly hedonistic.

Hunting and other recreational activities fall into the same general pattern of changing behavior. However, hunting ethics have certainly improved since the days Roosevelt began his hunting in 1883 in the Badlands of North Dakota. In those days there were no game laws and no government agencies managing any of the natural resources. Every natural resource was utilized or plundered for the economic benefit of man.

Various hunting organizations have their defined codes of ethics. The Safari Club International, the world's largest and most prominent hunting organization has an elaborate code, including concern for the environment, animals, laws, youth education, etc. Roosevelt formed the Boone and Crockett Club which advocated hunting ethics and established a system of keeping trophy records.

Roosevelt was certainly aware of the need for ethics when he said: *"In a civilized and cultured country, wild animals only continue to exist at all when preserved by sportsmen. The excellent people who protest against all hunting and consider sportsmen as enemies of wildlife are ignorant of the fact that, in reality, the genuine sportsman is by all odds the most important factor in keeping the larger and more valuable wild creatures from total extermination."*

To evaluate and simplify Theodore Roosevelt's hunting ethics, we can examine four primary issues, by today's standards, in determining practical, logical hunting ethics. These are: gun and bullet adequacy; shot placement and distance; bag limits and fair chase.

Gun and Bullet Adequacy:

Roosevelt was very knowledgeable about gun technology and ballistics. Records appear to be incomplete on all of the guns that he owned and used. However, much data are available on some models.

His first big game hunt in 1883 has been well documented, In September he shot his only Buffalo, two Elk and several Deer. For this he used a Sharp's .45-90. This was a classic rifle and adequate cartridge for any big game in the world at that time. He also had available a Sharp's .45-120 and an English side-by-side .50. This gun was very painful to shoot because of its recoil. He discarded the heavier guns for the .45-75.

Discussing the .45-75, he reported: "*The Winchester, which is stocked and sighted to suit myself, is by all odds the best weapon I ever had and I now use it almost exclusively ...*"

The author, shooting Theodore Roosevelt's model of the Winchester 1895 .405 Lever Action. Perhaps the most effective lever action ever developed

For his first Grizzly Bear shot in Wyoming, he used the Winchester .45-75. "*It is as handy to carry, whether on foot or on horseback and comes up to the shoulder as readily as a shot-gun; it is absolutely sure and there is no recoil to jar and disturb the aim, while it carries accurately ... and the bullet weighing three quarters of an ounce, is large enough for anything on this continent.*" Later, he would convert to the .405 Winchester, and be even fonder of it.

TR had several shotguns, 10 and 12 gauge. His custom made 12 gauge Fox shotgun was sold in 2010 for $862,500. In February, 1909, he wrote to Mr. Fox: "*The double barreled shotgun has come and I really think it is the most beautiful gun I have ever seen ... I am almost ashamed to take it to Africa and expose it to the rough usage it will receive ... I shall keep it as long as I live and when I die it shall go to my son Kermit who accompanies me on my African trip.*"

As far as shotguns were concerned, his son Kermit wrote: *"I have often heard father regret the fact that he did not care for shooting with the shotgun ... his eyesight made it almost impossible for him to attain much skill with a shotgun. In later years he never used a shotgun except for collecting specimens or shooting for the pot."*

In general, sportsmen, if in question about the adequacy of a rifle or cartridge, will use one heavier than might be necessary, rather than the lighter calibers. This was certainly true for TR's Africa Safari. He took an H&H .450-500 side-by-side, three Winchester .405 1895 Lever Actions and a Springfield .30-06. Other than Elephant, Buffalo and Rhinos, he used the .405 the most. He considered his .405 to be *"my big medicine for Lions."* He commented on the incredible recoil he experienced from the .450-500, whereas the .405 had very little recoil. I can testify for the latter since I also use one for hunting.

Fifty years later, in 1960, his grandson Kermit (there were three Kermits in that line) and his two sons would return and trace part of TR's African Safari route. They took one of the .405 rifles along with them. Their other guns were the modern calibers.

Not much is written about TR's use of handguns. We know he used two Colt .45 six shooters while ranching in North Dakota. He used a handgun in Cuba and in his biography he notes that he killed one Spaniard at point blank range with it. Records indicate that this revolver of unknown brand and caliber came from the sunken battleship MAIN. Since he was an officer and mounted, he apparently didn't carry a rifle or carbine.

In the spring of 1909, Lincoln A. Lang recorded that a dear friend of TR's by the name of Seth Bullock, from North Dakota, gave Roosevelt a .38 Colt on a heavy frame. Said Bullock: *"I send you today by American Express the best gun I know of for you to carry when in Africa. It is a single action Colt .38 on a heavy frame. It is a business weapon, always reliable, and will shoot where you hold it ..."* There doesn't appear to be any details him using this gun in Africa.

TR was very knowledgeable about the need for adequate fire power and had the means to insure he always used the finest of guns.

Shot Placement:

Roosevelt's eyes were poor and he wore glasses in a time in the West when men didn't wear glasses. This gave him a rare look and indicated that he might be a weakling. Nothing was further from the truth and records show he was successful in defending what might be construed as being inadequate.

However, glasses and poor eyes caused his shooting to be questionable at times. Rifle scopes were not used; only open sights and sometimes peep sights. This caused a lot of wounded animals to escape. He knew that he wasn't the best of shots. He said: *"I'm not the best shot but I shoot often."* Indeed at another time he said *"keep shooting until the animal is down, out of sight or you are out of ammunition."* Even earlier he said:*" "I, myself, am not, and never will be, more than an ordinary shot; for my eyes are bad and my hand not over-steady …"*

When using open sights, it is difficult to carefully place a shot at a distance, over 100 yards. Generally the hunter aims at the forward part of the animal. Using modern scopes a hunter can carefully place the shot, depending upon his ability, anywhere on the body.

Hunters, today, have sources to show exactly where the best place is to shoot the more dangerous animals. TR and Kermit killed 11 Elephants and none were recorded to have been downed with one shot. Today, the exact locations on the body are known and Elephants can be killed with one shot.

The first large game animal, a Buffalo that he shot was in the North Dakota Badlands. It was wounded and he and his companion trailed it for hours on horseback but never retrieved it. The next day he successfully shot another Bull Buffalo in the lungs the first shot. It ran, but being mortally wounded, TR had a chance to shoot it again to kill it.

One philosophy accepted by some of today's sportsmen is: *"shooters brag how long a shot they made; hunters brag on how close a shot they made."* Modern technology is developing a lot more shooters than hunters. Guns are available that are accurate beyond a thousand yards. The question becomes … how can an animal escape? This violates one code of ethics in relation to fair chase.

It appears that TR and modern hunters violate the fact that with open sights, more hunting and less shooting ability is required. Therefore, Roosevelt was guilty of shooting at and wounding animals that were too far away and more attention to stalking was needed. However, TR did record many times, on foot, that he stocked his prey.

One example was in the Big Horn Mountains of Wyoming, hunting Grizzly Bears. One evening, just before dark, TR and his guide spooked a large boar that escaped in the timber. They camped nearby for the night. Early the next morning they tracked the bear a few hundred yards to his bed. TR records that he got to within a few yards of the large bear. The bear stood up on its hind legs; TR quickly shot it between the eyes.

Bag Limits:

The decimation of the wildlife resources in this nation is one of the saddest historic events in the history of man. Greed and selfishness has known no bounds. It is estimated that in the early 1800's, forty to sixty million Buffalo roamed the plains of America. These numbers are difficult to comprehend.

Elk, Deer, Antelope also roamed the prairies, along with Grizzly Bears and grouse of several species. Waterfowl filled the skies and the prairie grass was as high as a horse's belly … but those days are long since past. The Buffalo has been restored to private and public ranches and refuges. The Elk have been chased from the plains to the mountainous regions. Their numbers have been re-established. The Mule Deer is in decline over much of the west. Antelope have been successfully restored in several states. Bears are only found in selected mountainous areas.

Most Grouse are disappearing, especially the large Sage Grouse. Waterfowl appears to remain stable, but never in the numbers of the past. Many of the birds slaughtered for their feathers have recovered and are protected in game reserves, thanks to Theodore Roosevelt.

In theory, modern game management dictates that the proper number of animals be determined in a given area, dictated by the carrying capacity of that area. Then hunting licenses are controlled so as to only harvest the annual increment. The hunting license restricts the number of game killed and this is called the bag limit. This applies to all types of game, fish, birds, etc.

In the United States, all wildlife belongs to the people of that particular state. State Game and Fish Departments are established to manage the wildlife, and make all decisions for the wildlife. This works well in some states, but here again greed, politics and the need to raise funds often precludes effective game management. This is especially true in Utah, where I currently live.

In the early days of this nation until well into the 20th Century, there were no game management agencies and no restrictions of any kind on the harvest of wildlife resources. Yellowstone National Park was created decades before the National Park Service was created. Until then the U.S. Army tried to manage it and prevent the wanton destruction of the wildlife.

TR went to the Badlands of North Dakota in September, 1883. He had never hunted large game before. He wanted to kill a Buffalo before they disappeared forever in the west. He was successful in finding one in a remote part of that area. He also killed Elk and Deer.

A few years before, a large party of hunters went south from Dickinson, North Dakota and reportedly slaughtered an incredible five thousand Buffalo. Is it any wonder they disappeared?

While operating his Elkhorn Ranch, TR would go out and kill four or five Deer or Antelope and then have hands drive a wagon out to pick them up. He fed his ranch hands on wild meat, as did the other ranchers at that time. Beef was too valuable. In TR's writings, he would report of his hunting and then would declare that the wildlife was disappearing in his area. One of the reasons for him loosing interest in returning to the Badlands later on was the fact that wildlife had disappeared around his old haunts.

During his hunting trips to the Big Horn Mountains of Wyoming, he had little hesitation to kill many animals. On one trip six Elk; on another trip four Grizzly Bears. In addition to these, he would report on killing animals for meat. How much meat could two or three men eat?

In 1905, in a letter to Kermit, his son, he said, while hunting in Oklahoma: *"The party got seventeen wolves, three coons, and any number of rattlesnakes. I was at the death of eleven wolves. The other six wolves were killed by members of the party who were off with bunches of dogs in some place where I was not ... the professional hunter Abernathy, who is a really a wonderful fellow, catching the wolves alive by thrusting his gloved hands down between their jaws so that they cannot bite. He caught one wolf alive, tied up this wolf, and held it on the saddle ..."* There is no account on how the animal was eventually dispatched.

On his 11-month Safari to Africa, he and his son Kermit killed 512 animals!

Many of these were being killed for the New York Museum of Natural History and the Smithsonian Natural History Museum. He and Kermit killed 11 Elephants. TR killed eight Lions. However, at that time the rulers of the colonies considered lions "vermin" and wanted all possible killed. This included Lionesses and Cubs.

More animals: 20 Zebra, 13 Rhinoceros, 10 Oryx, etc. It was necessary to have meat for hundreds of porters and other servants. However, TR doesn't detail which were for meat and which were for specimens.

TR had been criticized about the number of animals he and Kermit killed. Said he: *"Kermit and I kept about a dozen trophies for ourselves; otherwise we shot nothing that was not used either as a museum specimen or for meat – usually for both purposes. We were in hunting grounds practically as good as any that have ever existed; but we did not kill a tenth, nor a hundredth part of what we* **might** *have killed had we been willing. The mere size of the bag indicates little as to a man's prowess as a hunter, and almost nothing as to the interest or value of his achievement."*

The last big game hunt that he went on after his Presidency was a Moose hunt in Canada. He shot two bulls; by then, only one was permitted. His guide had to concoct a story about being attacked by the second Moose to prevent the ex-President from being indicted.

These accounts are not meant to detract from his incredible successes in protecting wildlife and establishing National Preserves, Monuments, Parks and Forests. It appears that he couldn't quit shooting if there were any animals still standing!

Later in life he began to mellow. He said: *"More and more, as it becomes necessary to preserve the game, let us hope that the camera will largely supplement the rifle. It is excellent to have a nation proficient in marksmanship, and it is highly undesirable that the rifle should be wholly laid by. But the shot is, after all, only a small part of the free life of the wilderness."* This was several years *before* his last Moose hunting experience!

Fair Chase:

The term "fair chase" was unknown to hunters in the west when TR started hunting. Today, it has a main connotation that the animal should be pursued in a manner that gives it a chance for escape. Recent scandals have shown animals penned, then released with the shooter nearby ready for the kill. This is totally unacceptable to any hunter with any sense of pride in the sport.

Other examples of unethical behavior: animals are not shot while swimming; ducks are not shot on the water; upland game is not shot on the ground, etc.

While Roosevelt ranched in the Badlands, he was involved in hunting with dogs of various types, including Greyhounds. Various animals were run down and killed by the dogs or by knife or shot or clubbed after they were totally exhausted. TR recorded that Whitetail and Mule Deer, Antelope, Wolves, Foxes, Coyotes and Jackrabbits were "fair game."

Since there were no game laws and apparently no sense of fairness to the prey, Roosevelt accepted the practice and took part in it. One difficult part of the action was the necessary ability to ride well, which TR did and there was danger of the horse stumbling or falling into a hole. Today, no fair-minded hunter would consider such behavior. However, there are still those who run game down with boats, ATVs and other vehicles, including planes. In Alaska, it is illegal to hunt the same day that you fly to your destination to begin a hunt.

Some of TR's hunting exploits are hypocritical to some of his own writings. In March of 1900, he wrote: *"Alike for the nation and the individual, the one indispensable requisite is character – character that does and dares as well as endures, character that is active in the performance of virtue no less than firm in the refusal to do aught that is vicious or degraded."*

In somewhat of a defense for Roosevelt, we recognize that he was young and enamored of his perceived manliness and taken back by his own physical development over time and with great personal discipline. But even with some sense of fairness, a man of such intellect should have recognized hunting with dogs for such magnificent animals was unacceptable.

His 11-month Safari to Africa showed another side to his hunting. If you can ignore the vast number of animals killed, his behavior while hunting some animals, was outstanding. Several animals charged, including Lion and Buffalo.

He records their charging but in a modest, unassuming way. Having hunted dangerous game in Africa, I know how frightening some animals can be.

Before he left on the Safari, his old enemy J.P. Morgan said: *"America hopes that every lion will do its duty."*

Summary:

Although much has been documented about TR's hunting experiences, little has been written about his hunting practices, in relation to modern ethics. When he began hunting in the North Dakota Badlands and in other areas of the west, there were no natural resource management agencies and there were no game laws.

In this chapter, TR's hunting practices were examined through gun and bullet adequacy; shot placement and distance; bag limits and fair chase.

His earlier hunting practices included running down ungulate game, as well as predators with dogs and killing them with inhumane methods. He appeared to mistake consideration for his prey with a 19th Century sense of manliness.

There is great conflict between many of his public statements and his personal behavior. However, he is credited with creating the first National Game Preserves and adding to the National Monuments, National Parks and National Forests.

He was very knowledgeable about guns and firepower in relation to the adequacy of killing efficiency. His arsenal was constantly changing, keeping up with technology. He favored Winchester rifles.

Poor eyesight precluded him from being an excellent shot. However, with persistence and drive, he was a very successful hunter. His greatest weakness appeared to be his inability to quit shooting as long as more animals presented themselves. He didn't use good judgment in considering reasonable bag limits, although usually, he didn't break any game laws.

Another weakness was that he often shot at greater distances than was wise, especially when using open sights. He probably killed far more animals in Africa than necessary, even though his party was collecting specimens for Natural History Museums.

He realized, first hand, the disappearing wildlife resources needed to be protected and that game laws should be strictly enforced, in spite of his own hunting habits of the past.

BIBLIOGRAPHY

A FREE AND HARDY LIFE, Clay Jenkinson, The Dakota Institute Press 2011

AFRICAN GAME TRAILS, Theodore Roosevelt, Paladium Press (Reprinted) 1999

A SENTIMENTAL SAFARI, Kermit Roosevelt, Jr., Alfred A. Knopf, 1963

COLONEL ROOSEVELT, Edmund Morris, Random House, 2010

HUNTING TRIPS OF A RANCHMAN, Theodore Roosevelt, Paladium Press Reprinted) 1999

IN TRACE OF TR, Dan Aadland, University of Nebraska Press, 2010

RANCHING WITH ROOSEVELT, Lincoln A. Lang, J.B. Lippincott Co., 1926

RANCH LIFE AND THE HUNTING TRAIL, Theodore Roosevelt, Paladium Press (Reprinted) 1999

ROUGH RIDERS, Theodore Roosevelt, Dover Publications, Inc., (Reprinted) 2006

THE HAPPY HUNTING GROUNDS, Kermit Roosevelt, Barnes and Noble Books (Reprinted) 2004

THEODORE ROOSEVELT CYCLOPEDIA, Albert Bushnell Hart (Editor) Roosevelt Memorial Association, 1941

THEODORE ROOSEVELT'S LETTERS TO HIS CHILDREN, Joseph Bucklin Bishop (Editor) Charles Scribner's Sons, 1929

THE WILDERNESS HUNTER, Theodore Roosevelt, Paladium Press (Reprinted) 1999

THE WILDERNESS WARRIOR, Douglas Brinkley, Harper Perennial, 2009

Time Passes; Will You?*

It was a warm, spring day in 1948. I was sitting in the second row of V.Y. Russell's American History class. Actually, it wasn't a history class; it was more of a history of V.Y. Russell, since he seldom talked about anything but himself.

It took me years before I would appreciate American History, after his poor performance as a teacher. The classroom clock was in the back of the room. I didn't have a watch and so I looked back several times. Would the bell ever ring? Suddenly Russell looked at me and said: *"Mr. Mahaffey, Time passes; will you?"*

I did pass and so has time ... 64 years. It's difficult for me to realize that I am old. I don't feel mentally old but as I look at my body, I realize that it must have been at least 64 years.

I haven't kept up with any of my classmates. I was a loner and had few, if any friends. I was terribly insecure because of the slowness of my physical maturity. I didn't reach puberty until I was 35 years old. By then the girls had reached menopause. When I was a freshman, I was 4'11" and weighed 95 pounds. A stint in the Navy during the Korean War contributed to my growth and I eventually reached 6'1".

Other teachers had positive influence on me. Ethel Lindsey taught me grammar and correct speech. "You rear children; you raise corn;" "Can I?" asks if I am physically able. "May I?" asks permission." There are many other simple things I learned from her. I felt she respected me although most students didn't like her. She was a large woman, intimidating and strict, but somehow, I connected with her. She also taught literature, which I enjoyed. But I dared not mention that I liked her class to others. I wish that she knew that I would go on to do research, write academically, and author books.

There were other teachers like Daniel Deti. He tried to teach Spanish. But I didn't learn much from him. "Si, Senor" was about the limit of my ability. Many of the girls were attracted to him. He was handsome and had a mustache. Few men wore mustaches in those days. I used to be amazed at it, since I didn't have any whiskers. Later, I would wear a mustache for decades. Shucks, if old Dan could wear one, so would I … someday.

Since I was taking the college prep courses, I thought I would try Latin from Ruby McBride. I had no intention of going to college since high school was trying my patience. I wanted to quit several times. I would go home and tell my stepdad that I wanted to quit. He would respond: "You're going to class one more day." And so I kind of went to school one day at a time.

Now Ruby McBride was about 4'11". She wore high heels to make her look more menacing. She would stand in the hall and chastise anyone who might be traveling faster that a slow walk. She had an obsession about chewing gum in her classes. In class she would stand in front, rock back and forth and have us conjugate Latin words together.

Biology was a required subject. Willy Vandiver was the teacher. She was old, or at least she appeared old to me. She was stooped and sort of shriveled. One day during class, I suddenly hoped that she had life insurance since I wasn't sure she was going to make it through another lecture. This incident reminds me of a physics professor that I had at Colorado State University who broke his leg jumping off a lab table demonstrating gravity. Those lab tables were high!

NCHS had military training called ROTC. I took two years and then quit. I liked the military teachers and I learned a lot from them that would be useful in the future. In retrospect, I should have taken four years. I liked the uniforms and I was very particular on how I looked, for my own benefit, as well as any girls, if any, who might be looking.

I was never involved in any extra curricular activities. I delivered papers for the first two years of school and then worked in the circulation room of the Casper Tribune Herald. I supported most of my personal needs from this job.

I never had a car. My step parents would never let me use the family car. I secretly taught myself to drive. I never had a date in high school.

I graduated with something like a B average. This surprised me since I was a lackluster student with little motivation. I was 87th in a class of 275, as I remember. I enlisted in the Navy immediately out of high school. At the time there was a contagious disease infecting young men across the nation called "gontokorea." Although infected, I survived and became a better man because of my experiences. The military appears to make a bad man worse and a good man better.

After the war, I returned to Casper and entered into an apprenticeship to become a printer. By then there were two papers: The Casper Morning Star and Casper Tribune Herald. I worked on both papers until I became a journeyman printer in 1957. I was the first man in Wyoming to earn an apprenticeship in four years. The usual time was 5-6 years.

At the age of 27, with a family, I became discouraged with the apparent future of a newspaper printer. I began classes at Casper College. CC started on the third floor, west wing of the Natrona County High School building in 1946. We were told never to go to the third floor, west wing. Why? I often wondered. I never did find out. Most of the first students were WWII vets.

By 1959 there was one building for the whole college! They finished the second building and I had one class in the new facility. I worked full time at night and attended classes during the day. CC was a friendly, crowded place. My advisor was a Prof by the name of Lawrence Lofgren. He taught biology and gave me a good foundation for my further study in forestry. Russell Bender taught me to hate chemistry; but Willis Fenwick made physical geology come alive.

Perhaps the teacher who made the most difference in my life was an English teacher at CC by the name of Bertha Davidson. She taught the required courses in writing. She was demanding and effective. She was not a social person. In those days, it was fashionable for teachers and students to smoke in class. There was always a cloud of smoke above her head. She could lecture with a cigarette hanging out of her mouth.

Writing was not difficult for me since I was a printer. I recognized good syntax, grammar and spelling. However, she would always find something to criticize. I never got an A on an assignment. However, I did get A's for the courses. After class one day, I approached her through a cloud of smoke. "Ms.

Davidson, why can I never get an A on a paper?" Her response: "Mahaffey, your ego couldn't take an A."

At the beginning of the third semester I became depressed and discouraged. I had a good job as a printer. I owned my home and vehicles. I was making more than most of the staff at the college. Why did I need to go to college? I took my books to the small cage on the first floor that served as the book store and asked for my money back. The student employee told me she couldn't give me my money back but she would take care of it. She put the books on a shelf.

I worked the 4-12 night shifts at the paper. I was relieved as I slept in for the next three days, not having to worry about classes, tests and lack of sleep. On the fourth day at 9 a.m., the phone began to ring. I answered it. "Mahaffey, this is Bertha Davidson. Why aren't you in class?" "I decided to quit, Ms. Davidson," I responded. "You get back to class. I have a lot of students who shouldn't be here but you are one who should be here." She promptly hung up the phone.

I was in agony as I returned to bed. I was in mental turmoil all that day and through my night shift at the paper. Her words kept ringing in my ears: "you should be here; you should be here." By the next morning I had made up my mind. I would return to class. But what about my books? I had sold them. I approached the cage and looked inside. The books were still on the shelf, untouched. I asked the girl to give them back. I crept up the stairs to my classroom and quietly slipped into a vacant seat.

Fast forward 25 years. I was in Casper and thought that I would go visit Ms. Davidson and thank her for her concern for me. I wanted to tell her that I not only finished Casper College but had earned a B.S., M.S. and Ph.D. and loved to write. The English department was in a new building. I wandered around until I found the main office. "I'd like to visit Bertha Davidson. Could you give me directions to her office?" The secretary looked at me strangely for a minute and then retorted, "Why, Ms. Davidson died a few weeks ago of cancer. Haven't you heard?" I slowly walked out of the building to my car, with tears in my eyes. I have never returned to that building.

Throughout the rest of my college career, there was always a mentor or friend to assist me. Some were nationally prominent and helped me launch my several professional activities. I am reminded that a great teacher doesn't fill buckets; he lights fires. Even now, there appears to be a few smoking embers left. In life, we seldom have the opportunity to assist our benefactors. But we can pass it on to others. Isn't that the essence of Christianity?

I have a long family history in the Casper area. Relatives on my father's side homesteaded west of Casper. Relatives of my mother homesteaded land south of Casper. My step mother, Una Harriet Uncapher was one of the first graduates of NCHS in 1927. The building had just been completed and was a marvel of architecture. It apparently cost a million dollars; an astounding amount in those days.

My wife, the former Barbara Alice Proud graduated in 1956. My sister, Juanita Ann Mahaffey graduated in 1960. I moved from Casper the spring of 1961 and so none of my three sons went to school in Casper.

* This story was written in response for an article honoring the 60th reunion of the graduating class of Natrona County High School, 2010, Casper, Wyoming

Wheels – Wheels – Wheels

Changes in technology in the transportation industry have been phenomenal during my lifetime. In my youth, there were no seat belts, turn signals, automatic transmissions, air conditioning or 4-wheel drive. Ford Motor Company had a V-8 in the early 1930's but GM didn't come out with one until 1955. Many brands have come and gone: Edsel, Kaiser, Fraser, Kaiser-Frazer, Oldsmobile, Tucker, AMC Ramblers, DeSoto and many others.

Driver's licenses are now a common law. When I started driving in Wyoming they were not required. Learner's permits, vision tests, insurance requirements and other laws didn't exist. Driving was more dangerous then. Radial tires had not been invented and bias tires often blew out, causing cars and trucks to overturn. If you could get 5,000 miles on a set of tires, you were pleased.

I learned to drive in a 1937 Ford Pickup, with a standard transmission. I was working for a few weeks at a dairy farm a few miles out of Pinedale, Wyoming. I knew nothing about driving, dairy cows or anything else, for that matter. The farm was owned and operated by a widow. World War II was raging and there were no men to work. She asked me: "Can you drive? " I responded, "no, but I'll try if you teach me." The widow said: "There's the pickup, get in it and drive." She used the same philosophy for driving the tractor and other equipment around the place.

Many people have love affairs with their cars, motorcycles or trucks. I am no different. In fact, sometimes I almost have a personal relationship with a particular vehicle. I presently drive a 1993 GMC Coachmen, Class B Motor home. It's a 1-ton van converted to a fully equipped motor home. There were only a few manufactured of this model and I am fortunate to still have one in good condition.

A recent venture took me to northern Idaho for a turkey hunt and then a return by way of Oregon, Nevada, California, Arizona, Utah and Colorado. I toured five National Parks. The van performed magnificently; with one exception: I couldn't pass up a gas station without having to stop and fill. I don't think it has a carburetor. It just has a large funnel from the gas tank directly into eight large cylinders.

It's common for people to name their ships and boats with female names. I don't know why their gender is female, but I like the idea. However, my boat's name is "Hook 'n Cook." Recently, I decided to name my Van "My Gal." Sometimes, in my senility, I even talk to her, but I don't want most people to know this.

I never had a car during high school. By the time I got a bicycle, most of the guys were getting old cars. In those days, it was very uncommon for a girl, in high school to own a car. I never had a formal date in high school since I never had a car. I never asked to borrow one. I assumed the answer would be "no."

My stepdad, Dave Mahaffey, was in the plumbing business and had several work trucks. In those days, they were called panels. Now, they are called vans. He purchased a 1948 International van; manual transmission, without synchromesh. It was hard to drive. Sometimes, I just drove around in third gear! I used to pick up a girl that I knew and we would go riding here and there. Dave had a small farm out of town and I was supposed to drive out there to do chores.

He found out that I was driving a girl around in the truck. He didn't say anything to me but the next time I got in the truck, I noticed that the passenger seat was missing! Not to be discouraged, I found a large block of wood and we used that for a passenger seat. Seat belts were not required in those days!

My last year in the Navy, I saved my money to buy a new car. I saved up $800. I sent it to Dave shortly before I was discharged. He and Una were living in Idaho at the time. It was waiting for me one day when I went home on leave. It was a 1953 Chevrolet 5-passenger coupe and only had two doors.

I spruced it up with a sun visor, fender skirts and white sidewall tires. The cost of the base car was $1700. It was equipped with a straight-6 engine and a manual transmission. Automatic transmissions were just coming out and were not perfected. The GMC transmission was called "Power Glide." Those who owned one called it "Slip 'n Slide."

I had a few weeks until I was discharged from the Navy. I took the Chevy back to California with me. One night, while traveling from Phoenix to San Diego, I broadsided a Ford Station Wagon towing another Ford Station Wagon, making a U-turn in the middle of the highway. I was terribly upset, but that was just the beginning of the repairs on that car. In two or three years, I didn't know what part of the car was original.

The Courtship Car

When I returned to Casper, Wyoming, in the fall of 1953, I was driving the 1953 Chevrolet. It was a neat car and few of them were around. I became an apprentice printer, and made very little money. It took what little I made to survive and so I used my G.I. Bill benefits to pay for the car. My monthly stipend was $70; my car payment happened to be $70.

Barbara and I dated for nine months, using that car. We could be easily identified but that was not desirable, since Barbara was only 16-years-old at the time and her mother didn't particularly trust me; probably for good reasons. We learned to use the alleys around town and could dodge a garbage can of any size.

Barbara and the Author in front of the courtship car.
A 1953 Chevrolet 5-passenger coupe.

After Barbara and I married, I was working at the Casper Tribune Herald, the local newspaper. I worked five days and Saturday night until about midnight. Barbara would occasionally keep the car and pick me up at the end of the shift. She would pull into the narrow alley at the back door and wait for me. One night she was sitting there, in the car, and felt a loud crash. The city street sweeper had banged her going by. She couldn't get his attention. She didn't know what to do. Before she realized it, here he came again and hit the car again in the same place.

By this time, I was out the door and stopped the street sweeper driver. He turned out to be an old man, blind in one eye! We looked at the car and were distressed. I talked to the city officials but they had no insurance. They finally agreed to repair it at the city shop. When it was finished, it looked as if it had been repaired at a city shop. I was glad to trade it for a 1956 Chevrolet 4-door-sedan. It had a V-8, manual transmission, with an overdrive.

Barbara and I have been fortunate in not having any major accidents, having driven for around 65 years. I had two serious accidents, with no injuries. We have never totaled a vehicle. However, Barbara has driven through the front of our garages twice; backed out of the garage twice, without taking the time to open it, and, recently, backed into another car in a parking lot. She felt sorrier for the woman, who had no insurance, than she did for her own damage.

The first pickup that I owned was a 1949 Ford ½-ton Pickup. It was a real dog, and I didn't own it very long. I have never had luck with Fords and I have owned several. In 1958, I purchased a 1957 used Chevrolet ½-ton Pickup. It had a camper on the back and a AC generator for running power equipment. I drove many miles hunting in that truck.

Saved By a Prayer

I bought the 1949 Pickup to go hunting. I had drawn a special elk permit for a rugged area just outside Dubois, Wyoming. Three of us went up to Jackson Hole first, to hunt in the general area. We didn't have any luck there so we decided to go into the special hunt area with my permit. We stopped at a ranch for directions and they told us to go 10 miles up a long pass into the hunting area.

We came to a large creek. I saw that other trucks had been fording it successfully, so I didn't hesitate in driving off into the current. I couldn't tell how deep the water was. This truck was 2-wheel-drive. Four wheel drives were not available, except surplus military vehicles.

We were moving across fine, until the water became about 20 inches deep and the boulders became increasingly larger. Suddenly, the truck could go no further; we were stuck. Water was coming across the floor boards inside.

I asked the two passengers to get out and push. They took off their boots and tried; I took off my boots and tried. The water was clear, cold and very uncomfortable. As we looked at the bank across the river we were striving to reach, it became apparent that no truck has passed by for several days.

I was not a member of the Church of Jesus Christ of Latter-Day Saints at that time but the other two hunters were. One companion said: "The only thing to do is say a prayer." I was distraught enough not to challenge the idea. So, we let down the tailgate on that old truck, leaned on it and said a prayer. We quickly moved to get back in the truck. The water was over our knees.

I had just climbed into the cab when I heard an engine behind me. I looked and there was an old Army Power Wagon, 4x4 Truck, with a winch entering the creek. In a few minutes the driver had winched us backward out of the water. I know that prayers are answered, but the speed of that answer may have set a world record.

We decided to go in a different direction. I killed my first elk on that trip. The year was 1956. By the time we returned to Casper, the old Ford was beginning shake, rattle and roll and died as I parked in front of the house.

GMC didn't make a V-8 engine in cars until 1955. Until then the engines were straight 6's and 8's. The smaller cars had six cylinder and the larger cars the eight cylinder engines. They both were good engines. I never owned a car with the larger engine.

Tires were totally different before radials came out. They were called bias tread tires. The better rubber compounds had not been developed. I used to get around 5,000 miles out of a set of tires and that was considered good. Now, 80,000 miles is common for the better tires. Blowouts were a grave danger, especially on a front tire. Barbara's grandparents were killed from a blowout in the mid 1930's.

I have no idea on how many miles I have driven in my lifetime, perhaps one million miles. I have never had a major accident but I have had a lot of minor dings here and there on my vehicles.

Barbara and I currently drive a 2008 Toyota Tundra and a 2004 GMC Yukon, both gas guzzlers. Several years ago I vowed that I would not drive a vehicle that I had to bend, crawl or contort my body to enter and so far I have kept that promise.

During the financial depression, beginning in 2007, GMC went bankrupt and took a lot of my money in stock. Then the government bailed them out. The whole sordid affair disgusted me. I doubt that I will ever buy another GM product. GM (Government Motors) is the new name and they only make GMC, Cadillac, Chevrolet and Buick products now.

The choices in vehicles now make buying a truck an ordeal … trying to figure out the best for what the buyer needs. Several engine styles, short beds, long beds, and all kinds of cabs, transmissions and accessories. Cars are the same. Only now, to add to the choices, we have many foreign cars on the market. In the 1950's and most of the 1960's the only available vehicles were domestic.

Four wheel drive pickups or cars were not available until the 1960's. Until then the only 4-wheels available were surplus military. These were Dodge Power Wagons and the smaller universal Jeeps. Ranchers often had the Power Wagons. I have pushed cars and pickups up and down more than one hill. The earlier 4-wheel versions had manual switching. Now there are full time, electronic, shift on the fly, automatic shifting when needed, etc. Thanks for technology.

Trucks That I Have Owned

1949 Ford Pickup

1957 Chevrolet Pickup

1965 Ford Pickup

1972 Chevrolet Blazer

1978 Chevrolet Pickup

1989 Chevrolet Pickup (Propane)

1994 Ford Pickup (Propane)

1996 Dodge Pickup (Diesel)

2001 Chevrolet Pickup

2004 GMC Yukon

2008 Toyota Tundra

Cars that I have Owned

1953 Chevrolet

1956 Chevrolet

1960 Rambler Station Wagon

1965 Rambler Station Wagon

1968 Buick Electra

1973 Buick LeSabre

1978 Suburu Station Wagon

1984 Jeep Station Wagon

1989 Chrysler Sedan

1991 Ford Astrostar Van

1995 Dodge Caravan

I was surprised when I reviewed the number of vehicles owned in my lifetime. Think, if I had only purchased half as many, I would be in much better financial condition today!

Man Overboard!

The Marines to the Rescue

The Author, a Hospital Corpsman serving on board the USS Boxer, 1952-53.

In February, 1952, I was assigned to the U.S.S. BOXER (CVA-21), a heavy aircraft carrier. I joined ship's company in San Francisco. A week later, we departed for a nine month's assignment with Task Force 77, assigned off North Korea.

I was a Hospital Corpsman with 22 other enlisted men and three doctors, one of whom was assigned to one of the aircraft squadrons aboard ship. All of the squadrons were newly assigned, as well as twenty percent of the regular crew. Each day we had various drills to prepare for duty with the task force.

We were operating out of Ford Island in Honolulu, Hawaii, for a few days before our final leg to Japan and then Korea. One of the drills that we practiced was the rescue of a man or men overboard. The drill was called "Man Overboard." Specific men were assigned this duty.

My assignment was as a Corpsman in the bow, starboard side of the whale boat that made the rescue. There were several others assigned, most with various duties in operating the boat. This included one officer, who directed the operation. A whale boat was a large, open bowed boat with an inboard motor. The total men assigned was six, as I remember.

The boat was attached to the side of the ship, just aft of the hangar deck. It was swung out from the ship with a large crane. Since it was several feet above the water, each man in the boat had a "monkey line." This was a rope attached to the crane above. Each man held to his line and let it slip through his hands as the boat was lowered to the water. This provided safety to the men and stability for the boat.

Even in moderate seas, it was difficult and dangerous to operate such a boat. Therefore, a ship as large as a carrier could back down in a large circle and create a calm for the rescue; assuming the man overboard was within that large area.

It was late in the afternoon of a beautiful day. The seas were moderate. Diamond Head Mountain could be seen on the island, north a distance of about 12 miles. The "Man Overboard" sounded. I was surprised since I had barely been given this assignment. I grabbed my first aid pack and ran up to the hangar deck and climbed aboard and grabbed my monkey line.

As fate would have it, an inexperienced officer was in command of the ship. The ship was supposed to slow down, and then back down in a circle, creating the calm. For some reason the ship increased speed for a short distance and then backed down. This created a giant swell, instead of a calm.

The monkey lines were not long enough for the crewmen to hold them all of the way to the water. They ended about six feet above the water. We had been lowered to below the end of the lines at the exact time the swell hit us.

The boat was capsized and then lowered upside down into the water, with the crane still attached. The officer's arm was caught in the crane and he was hanging, helpless. Several men were under the boat. I was thrown forward of the boat.

All of the other crewmen were given solid kapok life preservers. Since I had a pack on my back, I was given a Mae West preserver (Mae West was a famous twentieth Century actress who was amply endowed in places similar to where the preserver fit). Uninflated, it was a thin vest. It was inflated with two small CO_2 cylinders, each with a separate string trigger.

The first thing that I realized after being thrown over the bow was that I had to tread water! The pack was choking me. I finally pulled it over my head and discarded it. Then I pulled on one string and then the other; nothing happened. By this time I was fifty yards forward of the capsized boat. I could hear yelling but couldn't see what was going on. I knew that no one could see where I was. The ship was still slowly backing down and I was moving closer to the bow of the ship.

The water was cold but it didn't bother me. I didn't panic but I knew I was in a dangerous position. I was growing tired of treading water. I had all of my clothes on, as well as my shoes. I swam over to the side of the boat and looked for something to hold on to. There was nothing, not a ledge or anything. Suddenly I noticed that ahead was a sewage outlet. It was about eight inches in diameter. I knew if I could get my arm into it, perhaps I could hold on for awhile and rest from treading water!

About this time I heard "General Quarters" sound. This is a loud, constant call to man battle stations. Every crewman has a special assignment for this command. I then thought, "first, 'Man Overboard' and now 'General Quarters.'" No one will know what's going on and here I am with my whole arm stuck up the sewer line to my shoulder."

I could see all of the actions going on at the whale boat, but the boat appeared to still be upside down. It was hard to believe that none of those rescuing the crew of the whale boat could see me struggling in the water.

The call to "General Quarters" directs every crewman and officer to a specific location, with specific duties. A company of Marines was assigned to the ship. Some of the Marines were assigned to man two 3-inch guns on the starboard, forward of the elevator.

I was beneath these guns, trying to survive with my arm up the sewer line, hanging on as the ship continued to back down. Suddenly the ship came to full stop. The seas were moderate and the ship gave me some protection. At this time, I was impressed to swim out from underneath the gun battery.

I looked up … and there was a Marine looking down at me. "Throw me a line," I yelled as loud as I could. In a few seconds a rope splashed in the water next to me. Now, several Marines were looking down at me. As soon as they saw I had hold of the rope they pulled me up. I was so weak that I couldn't hold my own weight and so I fell back into the water.

I fell back into the water twice. Now, I began to be more worried. I was breathing hard. What could I do? Suddenly, I remembered back to boot camp where we learned to tie a boatswain's chair. A rope net for the buttocks. I couldn't remember how to tie it but it gave me the idea to put the rope around my body. I yelled: "more line!" I now had enough slack to tie the rope around me.

Whaleboats moored alongside the USS Boxer. The author was thrown from a whaleboat and nearly drowned before being seen and saved by the Marines.

Several Marines slowly pulled me up and over the railing. I fell, exhausted on the steel deck, face down. It felt so good to have some kind on non-liquid support for my body! Two Marines turned me over. "Are you okay," they asked.

I slowly sat up. "My Mae West wouldn't inflate," I said. I then angrily jerked sharply on both strings of the vest. Pssssssssst … the vest immediately explosively inflated!

After resting for a few minutes, I slowly walked down the hangar deck and below to sick bay. The Chief Petty Officer looked at me and said, "Mahaffey, where the hell have you been?" "You'll never guess," I answered.

I appeared none the worse for my experience. However, I did ruin a new watch and my shoes were destroyed by the salt water. I did get two shots of whiskey for my trauma.

No crewmen were lost during the accident. The Officer was treated in sick bay and then flown to a hospital at Ford Island. He never returned to the ship.

We never did have another "Man Overboard" exercise as long as I was aboard. That still bothers me. We never learned how to do it right!

SECTION III – HUNTING

●

Hunting stories about all kinds
of critters ...Scimitars,
Hogs, Buffalo
and anything that flies

To Kill a Hog

The difference between a pig and a hog is age and size. Any critter bigger than 120 pounds is considered a hog. There are different types of hogs to hunt around the world. In the U.S., wild hogs are usually called wild boars and come in various flavors and breeds. In some areas of the south, they reach huge sizes, approaching 1000 pounds.

I've had the privilege of killing 200 pound Warthogs in Africa and the smaller 125 pound wild boars in Australia. So, recently, when a friend mentioned I could hunt cross-bred boars in Neola, Utah, a few miles from here, I perked up and booked a hunt with Mike Richens, a local outfitter. A friend, Ken Harding, came along to resuscitate me or treat any deep cuts or bruises. He also agreed to take photos.

Hunting in Utah is different from other areas I've hunted. We were hunting in a reasonably small area, but heavy brush, creeks and bogs added to the difficulty. It doesn't take a boar long to become a stealth animal in the heavy cover.

We decided to use the spot and stalk method and then, if unsuccessful, rely on hounds to find a critter. I soon realized that the spot method was difficult and unproductive; the stalking was even more stressful as I became entangled in vines, down timber and badger holes. Ken helped me across the more dangerous parts. My wife's advice, before I left, "that no 80-year-old man in his right mind should be out boar hunting" suddenly appeared to have some merit.

I was undeterred, of course; what dedicated hunter or fisherman listens to the advice of his wife? I wanted to try out a new 1895 Winchester Lever Action .405, with open sights, for close order shooting. This is the gun made famous by Teddy Roosevelt, on his 1909-10 Africa Safari. He called the gun his "big medicine for lions." I guess it could be "big medicine for boars."

By late morning, it appeared evident that our spot and stalk was not working. So, we returned to Mike and asked him to release the hounds to find a critter. Soon two hounds of unknown origin, came screaming by me.

I noticed that they had been dressed in some kind of black covers, sort of dog chaps. Never having seen such regalia, I immediately asked Mike what was the purpose. "Kevlar," he responded. "It's to protect them from getting cut up by the boars." "Do I need some?" I asked." "Not if you can shoot that there gun," he responded. Now, that didn't give me any confidence, since I had never shot anything larger than a rabbit with open sights. Hopefully, a boar, if found, would be close enough for these tired old eyes to see him.

Ken and I hiked back into the deep cover as we listened to the baying of the dogs. One dog was a young pup and appeared to like the sound of his own voice. He bayed at everything he saw. The older hound was more selective.

As we followed the dogs, we would go in one direction from their sound and then in another as they worked their way down the bogs and across the creeks. This was really fun until I realized that I was getting winded from trying to follow them.

Mike, Ken and I entered an open meadow with some large low hanging trees. "There's a boar," Mike exclaimed. Sure enough, clear underneath, in the shade was a boar hiding. The dogs were way off somewhere else when we spotted the critter.

The boar stood up. I had never seen such an animal. It was black and brown, totally covered with long coarse hair. It looked to be about 150 pounds. It was industrial strength ugly. Its head was triangular and its eyes appeared to be in the wrong place on the head. Ken and I just stared.

Soon, Mike had the dogs back and they were beginning to explore the temper of this boar. He would strike at them and then run and then the dogs would corner him against a tree and then he would burst out and head for the next cover, the three of us trying to follow.

Several times I broke through the brush and tried to get a shot off. The dogs were so active and so intent on harassing the boar, without being harmed, that they were in and out like Mohammed Ali in the first round. The boar would strike out at one dog and then the other.

Soon, the boar burst out and ran down into a small ravine, and crawled between several downed trees. Here, he made his final stand. The dogs were on him again. Suddenly the older hound screamed in agony as the boar pinned him against a tree. Mike looked at me … "I hope the Kevlar protected him," he sighed.

The dog slipped from under the boar and then began attacking from the other side. Mike broke through the brush, grabbed the younger dog and yelled for me to shoot as soon as the older dog was clear. I threw up the .405 and waited for my chance to end this fight. I pulled the hammer back. The gun barked and the fight was over. A head shot dispatched the boar as painlessly as possible.

Ken was watching the action and was so enthralled that he forgot to take the photos! Mike secured some straps and we pulled the boar through the logs and mounted him on a 4-wheeler for the return to the truck.

We returned to an old abandoned homestead building for some more photos. During one photo, I called the older dog to sit beside me for the picture. I put my arm around him. When I took it down my hand had blood on it. Upon examining the dog's leg, it appeared that the boar had sliced him just below the protective Kevlar. It didn't appear too serious. The dog would hunt again.

Ken and I loaded the animal in the back of the truck and we were soon looking for the meat processing plant hidden in hills somewhere north of Roosevelt, Utah. We finally deposited our trophy. I now have two questions: what will the hog taste like and can I find the place again to pick him up!

*A hard fought battle between the dogs and a hog
resulted in this dog being wounded*

Although appearing small, the hog weighed 150 lbs. and filled the front of this 4 x 4.

Why was I so exhausted?

Is Fair Chase Possible in Nebraska?

I couldn't keep up. Kevin Shope disappeared into the brush! I had the camera and was supposed to be documenting the stalk. I stood a few minutes to catch my breath and then slowly followed behind him.

I looked ahead and watched as he slunk down into the branches of a downed tree. I was 50 yards down the canyon. Then I saw the huge Mouflon Ram moving into the wind and approaching Kevin. The Ram was limping apparently from a recent fight with a larger Ram. Another Ram nearby was more cautious and refused to follow.

This was another of several unsuccessful stalks for Kevin to kill a large Ram with a bow. On one stalk he even struck a Barbados Ram in the horn, without success. After seeing this Ram, I settled deeper into the patch of weeds, hoping my new camouflage would hide me.

I held my breath and waited and waited and then waited some more. Suddenly I heard the musical twang as Kevin released the arrow. I jumped up in time to see the Ram stumble, catch its balance and move toward the nearest cover. It disappeared into the brush as Kevin gave me the high sign indicating a good placement of the arrow.

Wayne Braun, our Guide and Outfitter at B&B Trophy Hunts, soon joined us as we began our trailing of the animal. But first, we had to retrieve the arrow, since it had gone through the Ram. It was easy to find and covered with blood, indicating a clean entry and exit.

The spoor was easily to follow since the animal was bleeding freely. It couldn't be far into the canyon. However, it took several minutes of following to eventually find the animal at the bottom near the edge of a seep. Wayne was the first to congratulate Kevin, since this was the first Ram to ever be killed with a bow on the ranch! Several hunters had tried over the years, but without success.

This was the second day of an exciting experience in the cedar breaks of Northern Nebraska, near the South Dakota border. My companion was Kevin Shope of Coeur d' Alene, Idaho; a dedicated bow hunter who specialized in hunting elk and deer. It didn't take much discussion to convince him to join me on this hunt.

Kevin was a great traveling and hunting companion, especially for me since I often need a little physical assistance here and there. Kevin is in his early 40's, slim, muscular and intelligent. He is currently recovering from wounds received in Iraq. Hunting appears to be a soothing balm to his physical and emotional wounds.

However, to my other hunting companions at home, any discussion of hunting Buffalo or other big game animals on an established ranch, especially on the plains and breaks of Nebraska, caused great concern. One friend looked at me and said: "You, who have hunted all over the world, are now reduced to hunting in a fenced pasture?"

And so, the subject of "fair chase" became an issue with him and with me, for that matter. What is fair chase? The size of the ranch has some indications of fair chase, but not totally. I have hunted on huge ranches in Australia and Africa. All had fences but the hunts were fair chase. This ranch, by any Australia or Africa standard, was tiny. Does that mean it was not fair chase?

I think not. One reason it had taken me so long for me to hunt Buffalo was the concept of a challenging hunt. I had killed the Cape Buffalo in Zimbabwe, Africa and the Asiatic Water Buffalo in Northern Australia and I wanted to add the last of the major Buffalo in the world to my modest trophy room.

Fair chase to me indicates an environment in which the animal is surviving and in which the animal can easily escape. If the animal must be stalked, has natural cover and can easily escape, then it is fair chase. These criteria were present at this ranch and so I decided to hunt Buffalo after years of waiting.

The ranch, located 40 miles Northeast of Atchison, Nebraska, was located in the mixed prairie cedar breaks, near the South Dakota border. Tim and Wayne Braun, owners, guides and outfitters were local residents and businessmen in the small town of 1350 people. These brothers were hunters and the opportunity to guide and hunt fulfilled more than just a business venture. They also operated a local meat processing plant and grocery store. The meat was assured to be professionally processed and frozen.

This was our second day of chasing Rams and Buffalo. The day before proved to be productive and exciting as I was searching for Buffalo but spooked various herds of sheep in our search. Several huge Elk bulls were spotted in the deeper ravines and a few younger bulls were grazing in the open meadows.

My intention was to shoot the Buffalo with my favorite heavy rifle … a Ruger .375 H&H Magnum, which I had used in Alaska, Australia and Africa. The rifle is accurate and deadly with its 300 grain bullet. I then wanted to hunt the Ram with a Ruger 30.06 which I have carried many miles through the years.

The first morning, after a brief orientation of the ranch, the four of us, Kevin, Tim, Wayne and I began a hike down a long meadow, bordering a heavily covered ravine. Then, through the ravine and up the other side, crossing a creek and through typical mid-America river. There were several tree species, including Black Walnut. The large husk-covered nuts were visible through the leaves.

I like to hunt with as few people as possible, but these three didn't intimidate me. However, four people make four times as much noise as one, so we were laboring under a sound handicap! As we approached the west canyon wall, Tim began to glass, looking for Buffalo, but none could be spotted in any of the open areas visible.

Moving South, through tall weeds and grass was welcome after straining up the canyon. Suddenly, a small herd of Rams broke from a small cover and watched us at about 400 yards. The four animals were very wary.

Tim turned to me and said: "Do you want to get closer and look at them?" "I don't have the right gun," I responded. A .375 would blow one away! Then, I reconsidered. If there is one thing I have learned from a lifetime of hunting, it's this … *take the animals as they come!*

"Let's get closer," I said. We crept into the cover and quickly moved South toward where the Rams were last seen. We emerged slowly and Tim ranged them. "Two hundred, twenty-five yards," he said. We were as close as we could get to them. "Can you hit one?" "Well, I can certainly shoot that far but the target is small and the gun is not a long distance gun," I whispered.

Tim quickly set up the shooting sticks as Kevin and Wayne got out of the way. I placed the crosshair of the 4-power scope on the shoulder of the largest Ram, which appeared to have a full curl. The loud boom broke the silence of the whole area. Each Ram jumped for cover simultaneously, including the targeted one. A clean miss!

I don't miss very often, but it was evident that this was a poor shot. My three companions looked at me. I shrugged my shoulders and said: "Let's find the Buffalo."

Wayne started in a Northerly direction across the meadow and led us across three small rolling draws. Suddenly, three more larger Rams broke from cover in front of us. Tim quickly stepped forward, Wayne and Kevin dropped back. "We'll have to hurry or they will be into the ravine," Tim said. Shooting sticks in hand, he loped over the first two hills and stopped short of the third.

"They should be right at the bottom," he whispered. We slowly crept to just below the crest of the hill and looked over. All of the Rams were gone but one huge one, at the edge of the timber. Tim quickly set up the shooting sticks and I dropped the .375 in the crotch. I noticed the beautiful curl as I again placed the crosshairs on the shoulder and quickly pulled the trigger. The sound was more muffled shooting into cover, but I was not concerned as the big ram was knocked off it feet by the concussion of the large caliber.

My first sheep trophy! Kevin and Wayne had been following behind and Kevin was busy taking photos as we progressed ahead. After field dressing the animal and taking a few photos, the four of us rested and admired the unusual color of the Ram ... brown, grey, with red guard hairs on its neck. A beautiful trophy.

"How do you want the meat processed," Wayne asked. "Well, I like leg of lamb, but that old critter is no lamb!" I countered. "He's older than you are. Can you give it to charity ... or Betty or Susan or someone else?" "We'll take care of it," Wayne smiled.

This Mouflon Ram had a perfect curl. This sheep may have been the first breed to exist, originating in the mid-eastern country of Iran.

As far as I was concerned, this was enough hunting for one day. But Tim and Wayne were discussing where the Buffalo could be hiding. The herd may have split into several smaller groups, Wayne said. "I doubt it," Tim replied. "They are probably clear over in that large meadow Southwest of here."

I wondered how far that was as I took a deep breath and rose to my feet. "We'll have to cross another large canyon and hike South again," Wayne told me. "Can you walk that far?" "I'm here to hunt," I responded.

Fort-five minutes later, we emerged from the cedars onto the largest meadow seen. Clear in the far corner, the backs of several Buffalo could be seen. The only cover was a large dirt pile and that was too far from the herd to hide us. We quickly moved to the closest point which was still 600 yards away.

"Sometimes you can walk straight toward them and do better than trying to crawl toward them," Tim said. We got into single file and began a moderate approach. The scattered herd immediately began to become agitated moving in different directions. Four big bulls moved in from the left. A large group began to move right.

I wanted a young cow since I was only interested in the meat and the hide. Besides, cows were cheaper! Tim was glassing but most of the cows had calves by their side and we didn't want a wet cow. The herd was now bunched together, but a calf-less cow dropped to the rear. The shooting sticks were ready and Tim said: "one hundred and twenty yards ... shoot!" The shoulder was large and the target appeared easy as I pulled the trigger.

All of the Buffalo immediately began to run to the right toward cover which was several hundred yards away. Wayne and Kevin were closely glassing the cow that I shot at. The cow was in and out of the herd as it moved Northeast. "The cow's limping," Kevin said and then later, "It appears to have blood on its right shoulder."

All were glassing now, watching for other signs of being hit. As the herd moved closer to the huge ravine, it split into several groups and disappeared. By now, I was very tired, but I kept up with the others until we could cross the tracks and look for blood. No sign. Tim traced one group and the rest of us traced another group into the canyon.

Thirty minutes later we met on the East side without and success in finding any wounded animal. After several minutes of discussing the issue between them, not without disagreement, Tim and Wayne decided to return to ranch and look for another Buffalo in the afternoon.

I wasn't concerned with the afternoon. I was hoping that I could continue to put one foot ahead of the other until I could collapse at the ranch house. *Fair chase? It had to be fair chase or why was I so exhausted?*

The weather was warm when we returned. All of the windows and doors of the newly renovated ranch house were opened as Wayne fixed our lunch. I propped my gun in a corner and sank deep into the nearest chair. A bottle of water and a rest of 20 minutes revived me to the point where I could eat lunch.

After lunch, Tim and Wayne discussed where the Buffalo herd might be found. They looked at me and realized that I couldn't do much more walking that day. Then Tim said: "I'll take a 4-wheeler and see if I can't locate the herd. But once they've been shot into, it's more difficult to stalk them." He disappeared out the door and I sank back into the comfortable chair.

About an hour later, I heard the drone of the Yamaha as it returned to the ranch. "Some of the herd is on the South meadow near Devil's Gulch," Tim reported, as I painfully got to my feet. "We can take the 4-wheeler part way but we'll have to stalk the North side of the gulch and see if we can get into range." "Range?" I thought. How about 50 feet?

On our walk back from the morning's hunt, my .375 was intermittently carried by Wayne and Kevin, giving me as much rest as possible. Both remarked how heavy the gun was. Kevin suggested: "Ben, take your .30-06. It's much lighter and you can shoot it well." "So, here I am," I retorted. "I wanted to shoot the Buffalo with the .375 and the Ram with the .30-06. Instead, I shot the Ram with the .375 and now the Buffalo with the .30-06?"

The three others were loading up and I had to make up my mind. I quickly went to the truck and retrieved the Ruger .30-06, crammed four shells in the magazine and climbed on the 4-wheeler. My energy renewed, I was ready to tackle any animal!

We approached the closest point to Devil's Gulch with both 4-wheelers. We walked a hundred yards. We could make out the black animals on the other side of the gulch. Tim led out, carrying my shooting sticks. Down the East side and then across to a trail West to where we could emerge, hopefully, within range.

Silence was important, as there was no wind and every step echoed with the crunch of dried tree leaves. After a few hundred yards, Tim left us and crept South through the timber. He quickly returned. "They're right there," he gulped … "too close!" "How can an animal be too close?" I whispered. "They'll stampede and we'll never get a good shot," he answered.

We returned to the trail and continued West. Tim and I crept through the timber; Wayne and Kevin stayed behind. I slowly moved a branch of a low-hanging cedar … there they were, grazing, totally unaware of our presence. What a sight! Tim said … "It's going to take several shots. Be prepared to shoot fast." "I'll put four shots in him as fast as I can," I told him.

"Don't forget, I want a young cow," I reminded Tim. He began to quickly glass the closest animals. They were moving in and out of each other at a grazing pace. "There's a cow on the far left and one second to the right, next to that large bull. Either one looks good to me." he continued. He ranged both animals … 110 yards.

While he described the animals, I crammed a shell in the chamber and placed the gun on the shooting sticks. I was ready! "Take the first cow that works clear of the other animals." Tim whispered. Then he watched …"Take the right one, no the left one is clear, no she's not clear now, take the right one." This went on four a couple of minutes. I could have put a blister on the barrel of my gun moving it back and forth!

Finally, the cow on the right moved clear. "Four shots? Four shots?" I thought. I slowly placed the crosshair at the base of the head, on the neck and slowly pulled the trigger. The next thing I saw was four legs in the air as the large animal collapsed instantly. Tim looked at me with surprise. "I don't always miss," I told him. The herd bolted and ran in all directions.

My young cow turned out to be older than I was. However, it was a great shot and some of the meat was edible. Kevin Shope assisted me in the stalk.

Kevin and Wayne were now beside us and congratulating me. I was pleased but I kept my eye on the cow for fear she was only shocked and would get up. Then, suddenly several in the herd returned to where she lay and smelled her. This was a touching sight to me as I had a strong tinge of guilt. It reminded me of four Cape Buffalo bulls protecting a downed bull that I had shot in Zimbabwe, Africa a few years before. The herd, seeing us now, quickly moved east toward cover.

As we approached the animal, it was evident that the animal had bled out well, with such a wound in its neck. As I looked at the cow, I exclaimed: "That cow is older than I am." It's hooves were long and curved and its body looked like a milk cow! "Buffalo look like this," Wayne said. "I'm confident the meat will be good."

The work began. The Braun brothers are efficient and organized. A large 4-wheeler trailer with a hand winch was soon retrieved. The animal field dressed and we were back at the ranch. It was late afternoon and the thrill of the hunt was slowly reducing my energy as I realized how tired I really was. What a day! The whole experience was not that different than days spent in the lowveld of Southwest Zimbabwe. Kevin drove us back to our comfortable lodging in Atchison. "You'll get a Ram tomorrow, Kevin" I promised as I relaxed into the seat of the pickup.

The pleasant weather, cooperative outfitters, friendly residents and beauty of Nebraska made the whole experience one that will not be forgotten. However, I was anxious to return home to Utah and sample the Buffalo meat that I had traveled so far to harvest.

The meat was processed very professionally, well labeled and generally, impressive. However, the first sampling of fried cubed steak was *not* so impressive. Why, that meat was so tough, I couldn't stick a fork in the gravy!

I like chuck roast, slowly cooked in a crock pot until it falls off the bone. So I put a Buffalo chuck roast and slowly cooked it for six hours in my favorite crock pot. I took off the lid and there it was … it looked like a combat boot left over from the Normandy invasion by the 101st Airborne Division! Kevin was polite and ate more that the rest of the family, but I was sadly disappointed. We ground up the rest and made sandwiches which were very good.

As I write this, I have been cooking sirloin steak for eight hours and it appears to be edible … wish me luck!

NOTE:

Talking with the Braun Brothers the next spring, they informed me that they had found the Buffalo that I had wounded. It was unfortunate that the meat was wasted.

Polar Bears and Polar Geese

Awesome Action in the Sub-Arctic

It was a small landing strip in Gillam, Manitoba, Canada. This would be my second charter flight, after two scheduled flights, to Nanuk Lodge, on the shore of Hudson Bay, 500 miles north of Winnipeg. I was hopeful of having a week's successful goose hunting.

"Where does the true Arctic begin," I asked a nicely dressed young man standing next to me. "About a hundred miles north of here," he responded. We continued to discuss hunting and fishing. I thought he was a service person, but he quickly said: "I'm going to fly you there."

"How old are you?" I innocently asked. "Twenty-three," he retorted. He would be the pilot of the large Cessna Caravan charter plane that would take seven of us and land at a short sandy strip outside the tightly fenced Nanuk Lodge. "So much for experience ... have faith," I thought as we packed all of our gear, including many shotguns. Most of us were taking two, in case of gun failure. I then watched a skinny, baby faced youngster help load the luggage. You guessed it; the co-pilot.

I was in a group, with six others, all from separate states, including Charles Arndt, Broker from Fin & Feather Safaris, located in Birmingham, Alabama. Charles preferred to be called Bubba, which seemed to fit him quite well. He was an affable, accommodating person, anxious to please all and have a successful adventure. This would be his third trip which gave him confidence from his experiences. Several hunters were on their second trip, which was an indication of success.

As the plane roared off the long, gravel runway, I began to review how I came to book such a hunt. It was 2005 at the World Convention of the Safari Club International (SCI), where I met Bubba. I passed his booth one day and was looking at all of the strange looking birds harvested from over the world.

I reviewed his literature and began to move on. I am not a high volume wing shooter, so had little interest. I'm more of a high volume misser. However, Bubba insisted that I give him my name and address. As a result, I have received almost as much literature from him as the National Rifle Association. Most of which I had little interest.

However, last summer, I noticed a rather obscure reference to hunting in the Arctic and viewing Polar Bears. My interest immediately piqued and we began several discussions, which resulted in my agreeing to go with him. None of my friends were interested, so I had to book alone. I met him in Winnipeg, Manitoba and we then took two charter flights to Nanuk Lodge.

On the way to Nanuk, we passed a group of buildings on the Nelson River. A returning hunter told me that it was York Factory, the first fur trading station in North America, owned by the Hudson Bay Company. Only accessible by boat or a short landing strip, it was not possible for us to visit.

The large Cessna had no trouble landing on the short, sandy strip, but sunk in the soft sand as the passengers and freight were unloaded. It had to be towed with a 4-wheeler back to the end of the strip, in order to take off against the wind.

THE LODGE:

The lodge consisted of several cabins and a large central building that served as the kitchen, dining room, lounge and three toilets with showers. Other buildings held generators, freezers, and miscellaneous equipment needed in the remote area. The plane stopped a few feet from the entrance to the compound.

It was, indeed, a compound, with all buildings tightly fenced with 8-ft wire, tightly stretched between 8-inch posts. The gate was large, accommodating the various 4-wheelers pulling differing trailers. For safety purposes, the gate had to be closed 24-hours a day.

In conversations with two Viet Nam era Veterans, each indicated that the fence was better than various compounds in Viet Nam, even though the Polar Bears didn't have rifles or rockets! However, our cabins were not bunkers.

Apparently, a few years ago, someone left the gate open over night and a Polar Bear greeted the cook in the morning. After frightening it out of the building, it had to be dispatched.

In addition to our group of seven hunters, there were three individual hunters and a group of three executives hunting and filming for the Drake Waterfowl Clothing company. The lodge is owned and managed by Stewart Webber with staff. All of the hunting was coordinated by Chief Guide Albert Genaille, a Cree Indian and other guides.

The lodge was built in 1977, but closed in 1990, apparently because of some family disagreements. Re-opened in 1998, it has been considered one, if not the best, hunting lodges on Hudson Bay.

The lodge staff was kind and accommodating, including the kitchen staff. The food was plentiful and adequate, especially the deserts. It could have had more variety. We had goose pie, goose a la orange, goose sandwiches and goose hors d'oeuvres. I was waiting for goose soup, but it never appeared. If we had stayed another week, we all would probably be honking.

Freighting materials into the lodge was very expensive. The flat rate cost was $2000/flight, regardless of the amount, up to 1500 pounds.
Beer cost $4 a can. I didn't see anyone drinking beer. At that cost, it could have been more effective than the 12-step program to help alcoholics! I did see a few flasks appear and disappear quietly. One night I noticed a few glazed eyes.

Goose limits were very generous: five dark geese and 20 white geese of any variety. The three hunters in my party killed a total of 219 geese. Earlier in the week, most of the geese were white. However the last two days were dominated by dark geese. The last morning most of the geese were Richardson. There was a large temporary butchering area. All of the geese were filleted, frozen and given to food banks. The remaining carcasses were spread out on the tundra for fox, wolves and wandering bears.

POLAR BEARS:

Everyone appears to be interested in Polar Bears (*Ursus maritimus*). They are fascinating to child and adult alike. Much controversy has just emerged as they have been placed on the U.S. Endangered Species List. Although Canada doesn't have them listed as endangered, the Manitoba Polar Bear Protection Act is very restrictive. No harvesting and no exporting are permitted. However, Polar Bears can be possessed for education or conservation purposes.

Polar Bears are huge, the largest of all bears. Adult males measure 8 to 10 feet tall. They weigh 550 to 1,700 pounds. Adult female bears are smaller. They measure 6 to 8 feet and weigh 200 to 700 pounds. The largest Polar Bear ever recorded was a male weighing 2,209 pounds. I suspect that if one was charging me, I'd think that he weighed the full 2,209 pounds!

Polar Bear cubs normally stay with their mother until they are 2½ years old, although some bears in the Hudson Bay area wean their young at age 1½ years. During this time, the cubs must learn to survive in one of the world's harshest environments. We saw one huge female with two cubs almost as large as she, so they would probably be weaned soon.

The Polar Bear is at the top of the food chain in his environment. Its main predator is man. However, Albert told me that three weeks before we arrived, he found a dead, mostly eaten, young bear. At first, he thought that it was killed by another male Polar Bear. But upon close examination, it was determined that wolves had killed and eaten part of it.

Apparently, several wolves will find a female bear with cubs, harass it until it is exhausted and then slowly separate the mother from the cub and then kill the cub. Albert put the remains in the freezer and is awaiting the wildlife officials to examine it.

Some scientists are alarmed by warming trends in the Arctic and predict that two-thirds of the world's Polar Bears could disappear by 2050. The IUCN Polar Bear Specialist Group (2005) reported that there are 19 subpopulations of Polar Bears, five were declining, five were stable, two were increasing and seven had insufficient data to make a determination. The reason given for these changes is the reduction of the sea ice. The U.S. considers the bears endangered; Canada and Russia both list the Polar Bear as "a species of concern."

There are three groups of Polar Bears which border Hudson Bay. These are described by the World Wildlife Federation. A recent study indicates that The Foxe Basin group is stable at 2300 animals; the Southern Hudson Bay group is stable at 1000 animals; and the Western Hudson Bay group stable at 1200 animals. We were hunting in the Western Hudson Bay Area. Other articles reviewed stated that these populations were decreasing. Whom do you believe?

As we landed at the lodge, we could see 11 animals spread across about a quarter mile to the west of the lodge. One day we sighted twelve in the same area. Some days we saw large single boars. The Polar Bear is a solitary animal and I was surprised to see such large numbers together.

I have seen many Alaska Brown Bears (*Ursus arctos*). I have always wanted to pursue one but never could come up with enough money go get serious about hunting. I have hunted the Alaska Black Bear *(Ursos americanus)* in the panhandle of Alaska. All three species are wonderful to study, and watch. However, the size, curiosity and aggressiveness of the Polar Bear place them in a separate class.

Churchill, Manitoba, Canada, is, perhaps, considered the most famous town in the world, as the headquarters for winter Polar Bear viewing. However, their viewing is mostly during the early winter and from large, special made, vehicles, to protect the visitors. A few miles from Churchill and a few miles from where we were located, is Wapusk National Park. It was created to protect the largest breeding populations of Polar Bears in the world.

We viewed them at a very close distance from the back of hand crafted trailers, attached to small 4-wheelers. Although all of the hunters were interested in the bears, hunting had a much higher priority, but not for me. I appeared to be the only person who had photographic equipment worthy of such an experience.

We saw bears every day as we came and went to our various hunting destinations. There were five different hunting parties spread out over a ten mile Hudson Bay coast.

One day, eight miles west of the lodge, my party was hunting on the lee side of a sand dune near the shore. In mid-morning I spotted a large boar moving along the shore line as the tide went out. The tide was not large but the nature of the flat land made a vast flood plain and the bear was taking advantage of it. He didn't see us and he posed no threat.

However, the next day, three miles east of the lodge, four members of our party were hidden in blinds along a sand dune. Parallel to this dune and adjacent to the shore line was another dune. A large bear was moving parallel to the hunter until he caught their scent. He began to stand up and wonder where they were.

The bears didn't appear to be frightened of individuals, but they didn't like the noise of the 4-wheelers. About this time, Albert, our guide, came by, noticed the bear and frightened him away. My party was a mile away and knew nothing of their experience.

There was one hunter who had been coming to the lodge since it re-opened in 1998. He indicated that he was seeing many more bears each year and they posed a much greater threat to the hunters than in past years.

One evening, just before dark, I was cleaning my shotgun, when a fellow hunter came busting through our cabin door and cried: "There's a bear outside our cabin." Indeed, there was a bear right outside but by the time I grabbed my camera he had retreated into the brush and was occasionally watching us by standing on his hind legs and peering at us.

Although our hunting success was as good as it could have been, the presence of the Polar Bears added an exciting and dangerous aspect to hunting in the Arctic brush.

Incredible numbers of snow and dark geese congregate on Hudson Bay before migrating south. The presence of large numbers of Polar Bears caused us to be alert whenever outside the protective compound.

GOOSE HEAVEN:

Having lived in mid-America, and hunting in Texas, Kansas, Nebraska and other goose states, large flights of geese were not new to me. However, vast flights of geese took on a new meaning. The presence of several species as well as the incredible numbers almost numbed my senses. Over a week's time, each new north wind would stimulate vast flocks of high flying geese that would last for hours at a time.

The moon was full and on cloudless nights, the noise of the geese all around us caused a loud symphony of blended calls of every description. On some nights that would be the last sound I heard as my old tired and battered body rested for the next day's adventure.

There were thirteen hunters in camp. We were divided into five hunting groups with various combinations of guides. Each group had a 4-wheeler with a large trailer on the back, seating from three to six hunters, decoys and other gear.

Our hunting was done in crude makeshift blinds, any available brush and in the limited timber that existed here and there. We changed locations often, which added greatly to the success and challenge of shooting six species or varieties of geese.

The variety of geese during the week was outstanding: Snows, Blues (Snow), Ross, Eagle Heads (snow), Canada and Richardson. The Richardson is a beautiful miniature Canada with a slightly different head. The Ross is a dainty, small white goose, very popular with some northern hunters.

We used one dimension cardboard decoys for the white geese and full bodied decoys for the dark geese. Although the flocks contained many young geese, there were enough older, experienced geese, to make decoying difficult. The dark geese decoyed better and flew lower than the whites.

It was surprising to see few ducks. There were some larger migratory flights at times. On a couple of days singles and pairs would fly by and look at our decoys. Warren was the only hunter in our group who shot them. Pintails appeared to be the only species available. I didn't shoot any. I was having a hard enough time shooting geese.

Since I booked without friends, I was randomly joined with two other hunters who came by themselves: Warren Bitter from Rockport, Texas and Jed Brusseau, from Carmel, California. The hunters at the lodge were not general hunters; they were wing shooting specialists. I immediately found myself at a great disadvantage. I am a general hunter. i.e., I hunt many different birds and animals. Therefore, I could not compete with these two incredibly good marksmen.

However, I adapted as best that I could. I shot the larger flocks and let the other men compete for the singles, pairs and triples. They would have them on the ground before I could get a shot off! They were competent at 65 yards; I am average at 40 yards. However, twice, while hunting by myself, I performed much better, without intense competition.

These two companions were the best shots with whom I have the pleasure to hunt. Three times Warren got two geese with one shot, both white and dark geese. I had never seen a "two-for" on geese!

Hunting geese is an art form for many, and they take it very seriously. Since I am not that dedicated, I had a chance to learn new information every day. Many of the principles that I learned were from my mistakes.

The various Fish and Wildlife departments, primarily the US Fish and Wildlife Service band geese and ducks at many points of their migratory routes. Hundreds are banded in the far north, near Baffin Island. These bands were aluminum and contained numbers and letters with a phone number to call to report where the goose or duck was shot. This helps the biologists in their research efforts.

Some bands stated a monetary reward for reporting. A few geese had two bands attached. The information about the goose after the first band was placed has more significant interest. Warren got a Canada with two bands. The second band had a reward of $100.

Most hunters were shooting various models of Benelli 12 gauge shotguns, using three inch BBs. One hunter had a 10 gauge, but we were not near him. Bubba was shooting an over-and-under. I also took a Winchester Super-X 3, attempting to compete with the Benelli. I shot both, but ended up using the Benelli the most, although it was new and I was struggling to adjust to it.

The last two hours of shooting before we left was the best of the week. It was very early and we were shooting small groups of Richardson Geese. They were not decoying well but were coming in low enough to make great shooting. There were few whites but they refused to be fooled by our three hundred decoy spread.

My return trip was uneventful. All planes were on time and my luggage arrived undamaged. Canadian customs agents appeared to be more kind and accommodating than the U.S. agents. Bubba took care of the birds that I will have mounted to remind me of this exciting adventure in the Arctic.

A Lifetime of ...

Phun with Pheasants

Pheasant hunting has changed dramatically since I started hunting them in the 1940's. After having hunted them in seven states, it is evident that the total range of pheasants has been drastically reduced. Many areas where hunting was ideal have no pheasant populations now.

This has been caused by fence to fence farming, rampant use of pesticides and the urbanization of millions of acres of land. Predation has been an important factor, including feral cats. The numbers of pheasant hunters have also been greatly reduced by the above factors.

I was introduced to pheasant hunting by trudging behind my Step Dad, Dave Mahaffey, as he hunted in Wyoming. He used a Winchester Model 97, 12 gauge. It was very popular, invented in 1897. It was a pump with a hammer. The safety was simply dropping the hammer down on the live round and then pulling it back when ready to shoot.

We didn't have any hunting dogs, hence it was very difficult to find the birds and flush them in range. Three pheasants bagged in a day was considered a great hunt. I was usually capable of walking for a couple of hours and then spent the rest of the day sitting in the truck.

By the time I was able to hunt, Dave had graduated to a Winchester, Model 12, 12 gauge, perhaps the most famous of all pump shotguns. He loaned his old Model 97 for me to use. Dave never actually taught me how to hunt, he just expected me to watch him and learn.

My first year of actually hunting was difficult. We were hunting West of Kaycee, Wyoming in the narrow valleys, surrounded by sagebrush hills and breaks. The ranchers grew a little grain, hay and alfalfa. Few people knew there were pheasants there and so there was seldom any competition.

I would spend all day walking, flush a couple of birds and miss. One day, about noon, after missing all morning, I was standing beside an irrigation canal. I looked down the canal and there was a bird flying toward me. I soon realized it was a pheasant and then I could tell it was a rooster. When it got about 40 yards out, I pulled the old '97 up, led the bird about three feet, pulled back the hammer and let loose! Two pellets hit it in the head and down it came. My first rooster! I was so proud. I noticed that Dave was coming toward me down a fence line. I ran to him and proudly showed him the rooster. He looked at it, never said anything and continued down the fence line.

After hunting in many different areas, the environment is usually the same, no matter what state. Grain fields, ditches, fence lines, canals, weed patches, etc. For many years I hunted with friends but without dogs. Then, during the early 1970's, I moved to Manhattan, Kansas and raised my first Black Labrador. I trained her myself and she was a good dog, but difficult to handle in certain environments — ditch banks. If the pheasants were running, I couldn't keep her in range. I've seen her flush pheasants, out of range, right and left for a hundred yards. In those days, shock collars were not available.

She was named Kate. I hunted with her for 10 years until she died of heartworms. I wasn't treating her for them because the vet told me that the worms were not present in Kansas. How sad and guilty I felt when she died.

She was a great dog and a family pet to my three sons. She was tender hearted and I treated her accordingly. One cold wet morning we were hunting pheasants West of Randolph, Kansas. I was walking across a creek dam to another field. There was a one-wire electric fence across the dam about three feet high. Kate passed under the wire, but her wet tail caught touched the wire. The electricity zapped her and she fell into the creek below. She looked at me with terror, thinking that I did that to her. She wouldn't get close to me for several hours. I hope that she forgave me.

For over 20 years I hunted with flushing dogs and enjoyed every hunt. However, when I discovered the advantage of hunting over pointers, I never returned to flushers. I have used several different breeds but German Shorthairs are my favorite.

A couple of years ago I traveled to South Dakota to hunt near Mitchell. That area is supposed to be the Mecca of pheasant hunting. I hunted several days, with moderate success. Actually, I was under whelmed after having heard of the incredible hunting in South Dakota.

Much of the enjoyment of hunting pheasants behind pointing dogs is their incredible ability. Here, the Author watches three dogs pointing a pheasant hidden in the cattails. We were hunting on the Pleasant Valley Hunting Preserve, Myton, Utah.

After hunting in Kansas for 25 years, I realize that it is seriously under rated, in comparison to South Dakota. My two sons, Clark and Scott hunted with me during their teen-age years. They both were good shots since they worked at a trap shooting range near where we lived. They often shot up their wages and came to me for cash!

One year we were hunting in Southwest Kansas, near Santana. It snowed the night before opening day and few hunters were out. A perfect day! The boys were prone to kidding me a lot, obviously learned from their father. A bird got up in the sun and I shot it. It turned out to be a hen, which was illegal. They began to kid me about it all morning.

My favorite pointer is the German Shorthair. However,
other breeds are great dogs to hunt with.

In the afternoon, I was trailing a pheasant in the snow. The tracks led to a large sagebrush at the edge of a draw. I could see the tail sticking out. I looked over and both boys were near. I said: "hey, watch this." I kicked the pheasant out, it flew directly away from me across the draw and I missed three times!

Speaking of missing and I seem to remember the pheasants missed as well as the more spectacular hits ... I had a lifetime friend, Terry Beaver, of Tekamah, Nebraska. He had a farm on the Missouri River and I occasionally hunted with him there in the late 1960's.

This was prime pheasant and whitetail deer habitat. We often saw as many deer as pheasants. Early one morning we were squeezing the birds out right on the edge of the river. We were tracking them and they were flushing through the brush and trees ahead of us. The roosters would usually swing a few yards over the river and then back into the brush. However, once in a while an old wily rooster would fly across the river ... into another state ... Iowa. The river was about a half mile wide at that location.

I was shooting a Winchester, Model 50, 12 gauge, a relatively unknown model. I had ruined it by installing an adjustable choke on the end of the barrel. I've since learned not to respond to new devices until they are tried and proven.

Terry had two birds but I hadn't ruffled a feather. Suddenly, right in front of me, a rooster flushed and went dead away. I shot three times and missed. Terry walked up to me as I was looking at the choke. "I think I'll adjust this choke," I commented, "Yea, put it on hit," he responded. Terry's gone now and I miss hunting with him.

Shotguns come in several gauges: 10, 12, 16, 20, 28 and .410. The 28 gauge and .410 are rare as is the 16 gauge. Years ago the 16 gauge was quite common, but is seldom seen today and the ammo is scarce, with little variety available. The colors of shells for each gauge are different to help identification.

Shotguns and ammunition have changed through the years. Some models have remained, basically, the same. Over-and-under, side-by-side, and pumps. However, the semi-automatics have greatly improved.

The first shotgun that I used was the Winchester Model 97, 12 gauge. The last time that I used it, the breach blew up, caused from excessive head space. It frightened me, but I wasn't injured. I gave it back to Dave. I assume he threw it away. Shortly after that I enlisted in the Navy.

One day, after returning from Korea, while on liberty in Yokosuka, Japan, I was visiting the Military PX Store. I never knew they sold guns. I looked and there it was, a new Winchester, Model 25, 12 gauges. It was a cheaper version of the Model 12, but had a solid frame. It didn't have a rib down the barrel. Ribs weren't common in those days. When I returned to the ship that night, slightly tipsy, the officer of the deck asked me what I had in the box. I replied that it was a shotgun and I intended to shoot every pheasant in Wyoming if I ever got back home. He told me to take it to the armory and that's where it stayed until we returned to the states.

The old shotguns had permanent chokes and the buyer had to decide what choke he wanted to use; they could not be changed. The most common was the full or modified. I selected the modified. This is the choke I have used most of my life. Newer guns have chokes that are internal and can be removed and changed. The more expensive guns have four choices, i.e., full, modified, improved modified and open cylinder. I ruined the Model 50 by putting on an external, adjustable choke, called the Cutt's Compensator. I was a great shot with it until I installed that choke. Faith in a gun is critical for continuous accurate shooting.

Recently, I was hunting with Craig Monsen on a Preserve. Before going, I asked him if wanted to borrow one of my guns, not knowing if he had one. He replied that he had used the same gun all of his life; a 20 gauge pump. "It's older than you are, but I love that gun," he told me.

He showed me the gun before we started hunting. "What model is it?" I asked him. "It's a Springfield Model 67, 20 gauge." It was well worn, ribless and the front bead missing. "I can't seem to be able to find a way to put a new bead on it," he commented. Now, I learned a long time ago not to judge a hunter by the gun that he uses. No matter what gun is used, it takes skill to shoot well.

That reminds me of a wealthy hunter in Africa who was shooting a $15,000 Dakota Arms .416. He was shooting at an Eland at about a hundred yards. After emptying his gun, he handed it over to his companion and said: "kill that Eland for me," which he promptly did.

Few hunters use 20 gauges any more. They are as potent as a 12 gauge but have far fewer pellets when arriving at the point of impact. As the day progressed it was evident to me that Craig's faith in that gun was beyond belief. A bird got up between us and went straight away. I decided it was out of range, but Craig pulled up and shot it dead.

As the day went on, we were both successful, but Craig won the prize for long distance shots. Faith in a gun is critical for continuous accurate shooting.

I traded the Model 25 for a new Winchester, Model 50, semi-automatic 12 gauge. They actually had a glass barrel or a steel barrel. I chose the steel. I have never known how well the glass barrel performed. I have never heard of one since.

I've since gone from gun to gun, seeking one that never missed! I've had Browning O/U, and Remington's. When my three sons were old enough to shoot, I bought each one a Remington Model 870, pump, 12 gauge. They cost $96 at K-Mart. One son blew his up and then I traded the other two for three Remington Model 1100, semi-automatic 12 gauges. Two sons still have these guns in addition to newer ones.

A few years ago I purchased a Winchester Super XII, semi-automatic, 12 gauge, and then a Super XIII. I still use the III and I gave the Super XII away to a friend. Now, I shoot a Benelli Super Black Eagle II, Semi-automatic, 12 gauge. Did you ever wonder how gun manufacturers come up with such masculine names? Just hearing the labels makes me want to buy them!

I've bought 20 gauge shotguns for doves and 10 gauges for geese. However, now I use the Benelli that will shoot up to 3½ inch shells. These longer shells have generally replaced the 10 gauge guns.

Ammunition has changed greatly through the years. When I was young, lead was used for everything. Now, all waterfowl in the U.S. and Canada must be shot with steel or some of the other heavy, non-lead metals. There are amalgams that are heavier than lead. I've used them but cost is prohibitive, for high volume hunts.

Recently, I heard about nickel plated lead for upland game. I am very impressed with them. The only company that makes them that I can find is Fiocchi, an Italian company, with factories in the U.S. The nickel keeps the lead pellets from being marred in loading and so the patterns are much better. What will technology bring us next?

The total acreage for pheasant hunting is greatly reduced and so have pheasant hunters. I am saddened by hearing that so many former hunters have quit. I live in a valley that has a lot of farmland. However, there are few pheasants anymore. Once in a while I see one. I am also told that there were vast areas of great pheasant cover but that has also disappeared.

Since moving to Utah, I have been hunting on game preserves. I have returned to South Dakota to hunt once or twice. Time, distance and costs preclude many such hunts. Preserve hunting can be fair chase and challenging or it can be ruined by poor management. I have experienced both through the years.

The last couple of years I have hunted on the Pleasant Valley Preserve, at Myton, Utah. It is located on a high bench with 2000 acres available for hunting. It is farmed specifically for pheasants and this is evident by the varied cover and crops raised. There are ditches, swamps, lakes, canyons, fields and weed patches.

*Guide and friend, Randy Dearth, praises his German
Shorthair for a great point and retrieve.*

The birds are strong and exhibit the same characteristics as wild birds. This has been accomplished by "imprinting" the birds with the fear of man. The birds are fed differently and can fly within the pens to help them develop wild bird strength and characteristics. Members can bring their own dogs and guides or guides and dogs can be rented from the club.

Although costly on the surface, when total expenses are computed, they are reasonable when compared to running around Utah or other states. When hunting with dogs, the hunter is assured of good *shooting*; whether the hunter hits anything is another matter. The season lasts over six months and provides a great challenge, especially during the cold, winter months.

Recently, I hunted by myself with guide Dale Johnson and two German Shorthairs. Dale is an affable and competent guide and his dogs are well trained. It was a difficult day, dry and windy. The pheasants were flushing wild and running wilder. We hunted three hours; I missed two and bagged two birds. This was as typical a wild bird hunt as you would find anywhere in the West.

Earlier in the year, a friend, Kevin Shope, from Idaho and I hunted with a guide named Tony and two German Shorthairs. One was a young dog, inexperienced and an older dog that was ill with some kind of stomach distress. The birds were very wild and had migrated into a dense swamp. We hunted and worked through that swamp and a nearby canyon all morning.

We were hunting in a deep ravine that had cattails and a creek in the bottom and scattered grass cover on a side hill. We had split up and the dogs and Kevin were below me. I was walking on the North side and found myself wading through a large seep, wet and slippery. I dropped down in the bottom. By now the dogs had caught up with me and were nosing around in a small patch of cattails but were not on point.

Suddenly, a rooster flushed straight at me. I shot automatically. He was so close, I decapitated him. I then started across the creek and fell in up to my knees. I had a difficult time getting out but finally extricated myself. I was standing there watching the water run off my pants and down my legs when Kevin caught up.

The dogs were still interested in the cattail patch. I said: "Kevin, there's another bird in there." I just made that statement when another huge rooster flushed. Kevin shot first and missed and I again shot the head off, since the bird was so close. Tony retrieved both birds and said: "Mahaffey, do you always shoot the heads off?" I replied: "No, haven't you been watching me miss?" It was a great day and we combined our efforts and bagged seven roosters. Kevin appeared to be shooting too soon and the birds he bagged were the longer, more difficult shots.

During the winter months, the snow gets deep, but most of the area is still huntable. Last week, a friend and I scheduled a hunt. He cancelled at the last minute. I was ready to leave so I decided I would go by myself and use Dale again.

It was a beautiful, bright afternoon with a temperature of 3 degrees above zero. But bright sunshine and the exhilaration of the day removed any discomfort. We were hunting in high, heavy cover. The birds were holding tight until we got near them and then they were running in the snow covered weeds. A bird flushed and I easily dropped it. "This is going to be a great day," I thought.

Another bird flushed wild. Another bird flushed straight away; a good shot but I missed. Soon a third bird flushed wild, but I got it with a sloppy shot.

We hunted for the next half hour, unsuccessfully. We could hear pheasants crowing in the windrows and swamp area. We moved in that direction.

A huge rooster flushed under my feet and I missed. We moved down near a lake and swampy area. Four more roosters flushed in every direction possible and I missed them all! We moved into deep, heavy cover where we heard recent crows. Dale suggested I hunt on the North side of a hedgerow. A bad choice! Seven roosters flushed, one at a time, in the opposite direction.

I ran as fast as I could through the snowdrifts around the opposite end of the area. I caught one last rooster and made a long shot in the trees. I felt slightly better but still disappointed in my being at the wrong place at the wrong time and in my poor shooting. "We've got to work you through this bad shooting," Dale commented. I didn't exactly know what that meant.

I was now exhausted. Almost three hours of non-stop trudging in the snow and cover. We were walking back to the truck. A rooster flushed wild and I again missed. We watched it fly across the lake and land at the end of a draw. "Can we get across that lake?" I asked Dale. I didn't have the energy to go around. "Yes," he replied and we slowly worked our way across the bottom.

When the dogs arrived, both went on point, stopped and moved around. The pheasants had been grouped there but had run in all directions. I moved across the dam and jumped down and started into the sagebrush along the creek. The dogs were behind us. I walked ahead of Dale. Suddenly, a huge black pheasant flushed and a ringneck behind him. I dropped them both. The dogs caught up with us and each dog retrieved a bird.

My success renewed my energy as we worked our way back to the truck. Dale said: "There will be more on that tree line, be ready." "No way, I'm going to quit on a winner," I yelled at him. And so six birds was a great day for me … even if none of them had their heads shot off.

Recent statistics indicate that in the last two years, total numbers of general hunters have been reduced 12%. I suspect that the reduction of pheasant hunters may be higher. As my eyes dim and my hunting days wane, I realize that without pheasant hunting, we will lose the stage upon which we teach our young hunters how to succeed in hunting … and in life.

Rocking Boats, Rising Tides and Grassy Beaches

Just Give Me the Bear Facts

Bears are fascinating animals. We are introduced to them as children in stories as "Goldilocks and the Three Bears." They are given anthropomorphic characteristics as "Smoky the Bear" endorsed by the US Forest Service as the spokes animal to prevent forest fires. The idea of "Teddy Bear" came from the media's exploitation of President Roosevelt's refusing to shoot a confined Black Bear. The media didn't mention that Roosevelt had killed several bears while hunting in the West.

Many bears are killed while hunting deer, elk and other animals. In spite of hunting for a lifetime, I have never crossed a bear while hunting something else. I have found spoor but never the live body.

During the 1980's and 1990's, I traveled to Alaska often, fishing and hunting, but never for bear. On one trip, while flying each day fishing, I saw several large Brown Bears, but never a Black Bear. There is a great difference between the Brown Bear (*Ursus horribilis*) and the Black Bear (*Ursus americanus*).

The Brown Bear is considered a much more desired trophy than the simple Black Bear. However, the expenses for killing a Brown Bear often exceeds four times the cost of a Black Bear. Many Black Bears are killed across the United States, but most Brown Bears are killed in Alaska and Russia.

But all Black Bears are not the same. On the islands and mainland of the lower panhandle of Alaska, Black Bears are huge, approaching the size of a smaller Brown Bear. The Black Bears become large from the rich fish diet and other plants that exist in the rain forest. After reading several articles about these large bears, I became interested in trying my ability to kill one.

Fair Chase:

The subject of fair chase in hunting animals is increasing in intensity and emotion. There are many "would be" hunters who only want to have a trophy and any method of harvesting is acceptable to them. It is difficult to get a bear permit in Utah, where I live. I have applied several times but without success.

Most of the bears harvested in Utah are killed using dogs. Some states prohibit this type of hunting. Some states allow baiting. Using dogs is a different type of hunting, with the primary enjoyment watching and following them in difficult and often dangerous situations. I have never hunted in this manner, but would consider it once for the experience.

In other states, like Wyoming, most bears, in the past, have been killed over bait or accidentally flushing them while hunting other game. I have talked to several hunters who have been successful. However, it is necessary to be hunting where general bear tags are included with other big game or can be purchased as a bonus while hunting other game.

The spot-and-stock method of hunting bears is the most difficult and the most ethical, in my opinion. It takes more energy in finding a bear and then the stocking can be extremely difficult in the brush or on the beaches. Bears have uncanny hearing and smelling. Although their eyesight is not as keen as other animals, they see well enough to require a cautious approach.

Included in the spot-and-stock method of hunting is the opportunity to ambush bears while waiting for them in key locations. This takes much time and much patience. Following the spoor of a bear with hopes of flushing one is difficult and unlikely. An exception to this rule is the method of following streams in the fall, in Alaska, when bears are feeding heavily on spawning Salmon.

Finding an Outfitter:

As my hunting and fishing experiences have evolved, I have been increasingly more cautious about guides and outfitters. This has been caused by some difficult experiences in the past. Buying a hunt or a fishing trip is one of the few items in life where the purchaser is almost totally at the mercy of the seller. Most outfitters require the total cost up front, at least 60 days before the activity. And, if the seller doesn't keep his word or conditions, there is no practical recourse for the buyer.

Recognizing these issues, I had never booked a bear hunt. I have visited with many outfitters at various outdoor shows, especially the Safari Club International annual convention. However, last year, a friend and colleague, with whom I have hunted in Australia, had a successful hunt with *Southeast Alaska Adventures,* owned and operated by Jimmie "Bud" Rosenbruch, of Juneau, Alaska. I met Bud and his family and booked the hunt at the 2007 SCI Convention in Reno.

Preparation and Equipment:

I'm no stranger to Alaska but I wanted to ensure that I was properly equipped, so I paid particular attention to the suggested equipment list. The most distressing item was hip boots. They are uncomfortable and difficult to walk in for any distance. I spent a lot of time getting the best fit possible. I had sprained my ankle and that added to my apprehension.

Bud wanted no gun smaller than a .375 H&H Magnum. Later, I was to learn that other hunters used various guns smaller. However, I had a standard Ruger .375 H&H Magnum that I had used in Africa and Australia, so that posed no problem. Besides, it's a wonderful caliber and usually under appreciated and under rated.

Since the weather could be wet or dry, cold or hot, I had to be prepared for all. It turned out that most of the time it was dry and warm, but I needed the cold weather rain gear on several days. Some of the other clothing items listed seemed a little excessive, so I reduced them. I learned a formula for traveling and recreating years ago: "*Plan your trip and then take half as many clothes and twice as much money!*"

Coming and Going:

I always worry about planning hunting or fishing trips without leaving adequate time for plane delays and lost luggage and guns. The hunt started on Monday morning. So, I flew into Juneau on Saturday night.

An extra day can be spent doing many things in Juneau. I chose to spend the afternoon at Mendenhall Glacier, a mere four miles from the valley where I was staying. A short taxi ride to and from made for a pleasant afternoon of wandering around the visitor center and walking the beaches.

Juneau is rather quaint, inaccessible by road. It is also strange that it is the capitol for the state of Alaska. It attracts thousands of tourists each day, during the season, brought in by large cruise ships. We saw several in port and then saw several as we traveled the main inland canal.

In many ways, Juneau resembles other seaports in Alaska, larger, of course, but attracting the same type of people. Most working various aspects of shipping, fishing and the service industries appeared to be poor. After reviewing the prices of all items, I discovered the reason they looked poor, i.e., they *were* poor.

The Alaskan Hunter:

Bud was supposed to meet me at 7:30 a.m. but was delayed for several different reasons. One of which was thieves had broken into his fuel tanks and stolen his diesel. We arrived at the marina at 10:30, where I was left to unpack and prepare for six days of cruising.

The marina was a deluxe facility, recently constructed by the city of Juneau. Our boat was moored on one of the last piers and was a little remote for carrying all of our gear. We took carts, packed to the top and slowly made our way to the *Alaskan Hunter*. This was a custom aluminum boat made in Seattle, especially for hunting and fishing. Bud's Dad, also called Jimmie, had designed the boat and had it constructed. Later, he sold it to Bud so he could begin his own hunting and fishing enterprise.

The boat was 37' x 12', with a capacity to lower the bow like the old LSDs of WWII. A 14' skiff was then pulled into the boat and used while hunting the shores or fishing. It was difficult to pull the skiff into the boat and it was all that two men could do. The skiff had a 25hp Mercury motor, which trolled down nicely but had the power to move rapidly when desired. The larger boat had a deep bow and could take heavy water. It was powered by twin 350hp Ford diesel engines. Under full power the boat used 12 gal/hour, which made it very expensive for the outfitter to guide one hunter.

Bud Rosenbruch's splendid boat for hunting bears in the Alaska panhandle. The bow drops down and a skiff is stored there for hunting.

Inside were the pilot's controls, galley, sleeping quarters, head and storage compartments. It had two comfortable bunks and quarters for two others. The seats were comfortable. The cook stove also served as a heater for the boat. The heater was never off during the whole trip. Its heat was welcome when we returned each night, usually after dark.

The sea life was incredible as we saw Whales breaching, including a youngster with its mother. We saw Sea Lions in vast numbers as they congregated to do what Sea Lions do. Harbor Seals were also prevalent at the entrance to various bays. One day we were under full power when two porpoises spotted us from a distance and caught up with us. They apparently wanted to play, as each one was swimming along side at 24 knots and then they began to cris-cross in front of us back and forth in a display of animal enthusiasm. I spent a lot of time on the bow as I could see so much more. It was like watching the discovery channel with a life sized screen!

The scenery was indescribable in many places. The rain forest, whales, dolphins and eagles were a constant source of awe to me.

The Bear With No Hair:

It was 2:30 p.m. the first day before we got underway. However, there was no real hurry since we just had to travel about 50 miles before starting our hunting. Although bears are sometimes up and about during the day, the evening, especially just at dark, is the prime time to spot them feeding on the beaches.

We would be hunting in large estuaries or bays and in other smaller areas that were protected from the main channel. I will not identify each area, out of respect for Bud's assigned hunting area. Some bays had one or often several creeks that flowed into them. In the Fall, bears are hunted as they feed on spawning Salmon, at the mouths and as far up as is practical to hunt. Bear hunting in the Fall is much more rigorous than in the Spring.

In the Spring, there are no fish available for the bears and so they are forced to feed on floral material in the timber and the plants and grasses on the beaches. Unknown to me, until observing them, bears graze on the grasses like cows and horses. They come out in the evenings and feed until satisfied, or until dark.

We unloaded our skiff from the boat and prepared to slowly and quietly move up the bay to the point where the creek entered the bay. However, the state of the tide determined how far inland we could travel. The tide is always coming or going and must be seriously considered to determine where to hunt and how to anchor out while hunting. If careless, the boat will be beached and it will be 12 hours until the tide returns.

We just entered the bay when Bud spotted a large bear on the West side. The wind was in our face. We slowly drifted ashore. Since the tide was coming in we didn't worry about the boat. We began our stock of 300 yards and hid behind several large rocks on the beach.

The Black Bear was out 65 yards feeding away from us. I was sitting behind Bud as he assessed the bear. "How are you going to mount this bear? A rug mount?" he inquired. "No, a half sized live mount," I answered. "He doesn't have any hair on his hips. He has a long mane." Bud responded. "How about his front shoulders?" I asked. "They are rubbed bare." Well, how about a neck mount," I retorted. "He's rubbed on the neck and has scars on his face. But he's big, at least 71/2 feet."

By now I had crept up and was watching the bear through my scope, placed on my shooting sticks. Bud could see him much better with his binoculars. By now the bear was broadside and looked like some character out of a Disney cartoon. "No bear is better than a bear with no hair," I laughed, "especially on the first night. We can do better, can't we?" Bud nodded in agreement and we watched the bear wander down the beach out of sight.

The next morning dawned bright and clear, very unusual for that part of Alaska that only receives around 15 cloudless days a year. The stream that we saw the night before looked promising for early spawning Dollies or Rainbows, so we decided that we would spend a few hours hiking and fishing.

Bud also wanted to show me the place where Stan Welsh had shot his trophy bear last year. The tide was changing but we managed to find a good place to anchor the boat and begin fishing. But before we could get out of the boat we spotted a black Wolf streaking up the creek.

Wolves can be hunted in the fall but not in the Spring. However, that Wolf would never allow any person to get within shooting range. As I hiked up the creek, I followed his tracks for hundreds of yards. His tracks were huge … five inches across.

The creek was beautiful, with clear, deep holes. The only problem was that there were no fish present! Some of the larger streams in Alaska have resident Dollies and Rainbows, but this creek apparently only had migrant fish that accompanied the spawning Salmon when they arrived. We were simply too early.

The Shower Bear:

We traveled another couple of hours at moderate speed, seeing several fishing boats coming and going up the main channel. Suddenly Bud made a sharp turn into a small bay. Ahead was a small, modern dock. I couldn't figure out why the Dept. of Fish and Game would build such a facility in such a place.

We saw no bears during our morning jaunt and had seen none on the beaches before arriving at our mooring site. At 6:00 p.m., we unloaded the skiff and hunted across the small bay and entered into a very large estuary. At the entrance was a large Dept. of Fish and Game Boat, apparently used to enforce the commercial fishing regulations over a broad area. It was abandoned, except for one deck hand who waved at us as we went by.

We watched for bear on several beaches without success. Then Bud steered the boat through a narrow canyon. The tide was moving so rapidly in that it had created a series of rapids as we entered another totally hidden bay. Ducks and Lesser Canada Geese were moving up and down the beach in an agitated sort of way.

Since the tide was moving in, we could get to the upper reaches of the bay, but would have to plan for the tide moving out in two hours or less. Bud had hunted there many times. It was a prime bear feeding area. However, after a long wait, none showed up.

However, after about a half an hour, Bud spotted a beige colored Wolf across the bay and then a second and then a third Wolf. I saw the first two but never spotted the third. The two were acting as if they were in some kind of a courtship relationship, while the third one watched from a distance, according to Bud. I was realizing that when the light was poor, I was having difficulty seeing in the distance. The evening of waiting produced no bears, but the

Wolves and the movement of several small flocks of geese was an interesting experience for me.

By the time we arrived where the rapids had appeared, the tide was rapidly moving in the opposite direction. There was a three foot drop off a ledge that we couldn't see. The boat fell over the ledge before I knew what was happening! It was a violent jolt as the bow bottomed out and then adjusted itself. It was fortunate that we didn't see the danger before or we might not have had the courage to try to get through it.

The next morning we continued South for several miles and pulled into a beautiful sheltered bay. It appeared to be about eight miles deep with several islands in the middle. We put out our Crab pots South, near the first island and returned to the boat.

I decided to take a shower before the water cooled down. The hot water was heated off the manifold of each of the two engines. There was plenty of water and it felt good to get clean.

I had just emerged and was drying off when Bud exclaimed: "Bear on the beach!" I laughed and said I knew about those jokes when hunters were in a compromising position. "It's no joke, look over there he exclaimed!" I dropped my towel and scrambled over the nearest seat to where I could see the beach.

Sure, enough, near a large rock, a bear was meandering around during the middle of the day. "I'll shoot him right off the boat," I said seriously to Bud. "It's illegal. You can't shoot off the boat." "Oh, watch me," as I made a gesture to get my gun, stark naked. He realized that I wasn't serious since I couldn't quit laughing as I put on my clothes.

By the time I was dressed, the bear was gone. I took my range finder and shot the rock where the bear was standing. It was 394 yards. "Don't worry," I said, "I couldn't hit a bear at 394 yards if it was as big as a moose."

Night Vision Goggles:

The next morning promised to be another glorious day of unusual sunshine and high temperatures. We had set out our Crab pots, with bait, the afternoon before, in hopes of catching a few meals of Dungeness Crab. I like Crab but I knew nothing about how to catch them in pots.

A 48-inch round, 12 inch high wire covered pot is set on the bottom of the sea. A bait container is set inside with some kind of rotten fish. There are two entrances to the center, where the bait is placed. Each entrance has a one-way flapper door. The Crab smells the bait, enters the door, and cannot get out. Our first pot was empty, but the second pot had several females, which are turned back and two very large males. We kept the males.

The next day, some other bear hunters staying in a Forest Service cabin told us to check their pot and use what we wanted. We caught eight large Crabs in that pot. We had enough Crabs to last the trip. The Crabs are kept alive, until wanted, in salt water. Then they are killed and immediately boiled in sea water, cracked and devoured.

The first morning of crabbing was a new experience for me. We just took what gear we needed, leaving our boots and hunting gear on the main boat. After collecting the Crabs and rebaiting the pots, we spotted a Forest Service Cabin on the shore. It looked so interesting that we made our way in that direction.

As we neared the cabin, we saw a very nice bear on the beach. However, we didn't have our binoculars or any hunting gear! We slowly cruised near the bear until it heard the motor and disappeared into the dense undergrowth.

I told Bud before leaving: "If we take our hunting gear we won't see a bear; if we don't take our hunting gear, we will see a bear. So, let's see a bear!" I was only joking but my statement was prophecy. Since we didn't bring our cameras or boots, we couldn't explore. I told Bud that I wanted to spend some time in the afternoon at the cabin.

In mid-afternoon, we explored the cabin, which was built for renting to hunters and fishermen. It was constructed in 1984, but had been renovated last year, cleaned, painted and a beautiful deck and stairs added to its charm. It had a log dating to its first tenant and all those after. I spent several minutes reading the entries from people all over the country and their experiences hunting and fishing.

Toward late evening, we began our search for another bear. The bay was quite large and offered extended beaches in several directions. We were unsuccessful but had not reached the last beach on the South side of the bay. I was very tired and would have been pleased to call it a day.

However, Bud would have none of that. There was still light. It was 9:50 p.m., as we approached the far beach at about 2500 yards. I glassed the beach but could only identify large rocks; bear rocks, as I began to call them. Bud slowed the boat down and began glassing. "There's a bear on the far left under those two large trees." Bud stated. I could see the trees but I couldn't spot the bear. "I can't see it, but if you tell me there's a bear there, I believe you. That's why I'm paying you," I yelled over the noise of the motor.

The wind was calm, so we could drift in and stalk from the West. I still had not seen the bear. We anchored out far enough to keep the boat in water from the outgoing tide. I got out of the boat and stated: "Bud, there's very little light left." He didn't pay any attention to me and started across the beach like a stripped-assed ape.

He was almost running, but the mud was slippery, and I had my gun and a shooting stick. I fell behind a hundred yards. Bud slipped behind a large rock as he continued to glass the bear. I came up beside him and was trying to see the bear in my binoculars. "Do you see him now? What direction is he facing?" Bud questioned. "I still don't see him." I answered. Bud shrugged his shoulders in a disgusted gesture. "These eyes are 75 years old and about worn out. I couldn't see that bear with night vision goggles," I said more defensively than apologetically.

By now, it was too dark to shoot anything unless it was within 25 yards on a white background. Bud went back to the boat and waited as I slowly returned. It was about 8 miles back to the mother boat. I had forgotten my jacket and it was cold. Bud loaned me his jacket. I sat back and relaxed as Bud cranked the boat to full speed for our return.

The One-Eyed Bear:

The fourth day of hunting dawned clear and cool. I was awake in my bunk thinking about all that was happening around me. Time was passing so fast. Four days and not a decent opportunity for a bear. Then I began to have hunter's remorse …"Was a bear with no hair better than no bear?" On the fourth day, the bear began to grow some hair in my mind!

Most guides are patient and forgiving … especially if they haven't collected all of their fees for the hunt. However, Bud was kind and patient and didn't mention my inability to see a Black bear in the dark. Actually, we got along well, in spite of my physical inabilities.

By late afternoon, we were back on the water, binoculars in hand, surveying every moving thing on every visible beach. Each day I was increasingly grateful for the outstanding spotting ability that Bud had developed over the years. He had honed this ability well and I began to leave the spotting to him. The bears are very aware of any danger and must be approached from a far as possible.

By 6:00 p.m., Bud had spotted what looked like a good bear feeding on a very narrow strip of beach. We were traveling with the wind, so we stayed as far out in the middle of the bay as possible and drifted 800 yards past the bear. We landed on a steep, rocky beach. The tide was changing; we anchored out a few yards for safety. I got out of the boat, put a shell in the chamber and adjusted my shooting stick for a walking stick. My binoculars were around my neck. Bud moved up the beach and promptly moved West into the wind toward where the bear was last seen.

We quietly walked bow-legged, to keep our boots from rubbing until the bear was spotted at 400 yards. Then we crawled over rocks, brush and barnacles until reaching some downed trees for cover. We slipped though these, found a small meandering creek and followed it until there was no additional cover.

The bear was still feeding in our direction but had moved behind some downed trees. We could see him clearly behind the trees at 200 yards. Bud slipped to the left for the best view. "You might be able to get a shot from here," he whispered. I raised my .375 H&H, but my view was blocked. I could see the bear but there was too much brush for an adequate shot.

Bud continued to glass the bear until it slowly moved into the dense undergrowth. "He may come out. Let's wait until 7:30," I whispered. Bud agreed and so we relaxed and tried to get comfortable. However, the ground was totally soggy and so we couldn't sit down. We crouched as best we could.

At 7:20 p.m., I began to get nervous, fearing losing the rest of the evening, searching for other bears. I suggested that Bud go back, pick up the boat and we could continue hunting. Meanwhile I would wait in case the bear came out. In 20 more minutes, I arose and slipped over to where the bear was last seen. At this time, I realized that bears graze like cows or horses on the tender grasses and sedges. He must have spent a long time feeding but we were too late. Before leaving he deposited a large pile of dung that indicated he was a big bear.

The bay was huge, especially if only one party of hunters were present. We hunted the East beaches until the bay narrowed, with a beautiful island in the middle. We passed by the island and then the bay expanded to a couple of miles wide. The only creek entering the bay was on the Southeast corner. We hadn't hunted that far and so we began to move in that direction.

However, the long, Southern beach loomed ahead of us at about 2500 yards, the same as the night before. By now it was 9:15 and my apprehension was increasing. Suddenly Bud announced a bear in the Southwestern corner of the beach. I couldn't see it, but I trusted his statement.

I thought, perhaps, that my binoculars weren't good enough in such light and that it might not be my poor eyesight. My glasses were Bushnell; their best small, hunting model. However, Bud had a pair of Swarovski binoculars, reputed to be the best in the industry. They are made in Austria, and are very expensive. The company also makes scopes and other optics. I asked to borrow his Swarovski's. There appeared to be a little better light gathering qualities, but I still couldn't see the bear.

Bud slowed the motor down to slow idle as we progressed South. We discussed how to approach the bear. The wind was variable, coming from different directions. "We'll go straight in," he said. "No, I countered." We continued on and the wind stopped. "Now, we can go in from the East or West," I suggested. We continued on and suddenly, a moderate wind came from the West.

Now, we had to approach the bear from the East, directly into the wind … a great advantage. We slowly moved East, keeping the bear in sight. I finally spotted the bear on a narrow strip of beach, feeding in the grass. I began to get excited; this might be our chance.

We slowly directed the boat into a long, narrow isthmus. Bud looked around and decided how far out to anchor to ensure enough water to get out. I grabbed my rifle and shooting sticks and flopped over the side of the boat into water 3 feet deep.

The time was 9:35, with plenty of light. Bud led out rapidly. I couldn't keep up with him; however, he waited at the beach. We could barely see the bear from there. I looked ahead and the beach made a contour inward. "We can go along the edge of the brush to that far point," I suggested. "The bear can't see us as we move." We quickly made our way over the rocky ground until we reached the point.

I guessed that the bear would be about 500 yards from there. I slowly looked through my Bushnell binoculars. He was only 200 yards away, grazing in our direction! Should we shoot from here? Could we get closer? I looked ahead about 50 yards and several trees had blown down on the beach and would make a blind if we could get that far without being seen or heard.

Bud led out and slithered like a snake, on one side and then on the other side of his body. My gun was much heavier than his and I also had a shooting stick. My slithering was very clumsy. I fell behind him several yards and rested often as we sought the protection of the trees.

Bud moved to the right and I moved up to the main tree. I squirmed here and there until I could make a decent rest on the tree. I looked through my scope and there he was! Bud *encouraged* me by saying: "Mahaffey, you're only going to get one shot and he'll be in the brush."

A couple of days before, we had a discussion that a guide can kill a wounded bear for a client. I said: "Bud, if you're so concerned, get over there and you can shoot the second that I shoot and then, technically, it will be a wounded bear." He had to think about that for a minute but then he agreed.

By now, the bear had turned and was grazing away. "He's going away, don't shoot," Bud frantically said. "I know the front from the ass end of a bear," I answered. Then, slowly the bear began to graze in a circle to his right and became what I thought was full broadside. However, in dimming light, a Black bear is difficult to discern detailed physical features.

I placed the cross-hairs low on the shoulder, without any compensation for distance, and pulled the trigger. **Whoomp,** the bear dropped like no other animal I have ever shot! A second after I shot, Bud shot. But it was too late, the bear was down. We watched for a minute. There was no sign of any further movement.

I breathed a sigh of relief. A great shot! The Ruger .375 H&H Magnum had performed well, as it has always performed for me. We slowly approached the bear. I put another shell in the chamber and asked if I should shoot it again. Bud said "no", as he walked around the bear. "Mahaffey, you have a world class trophy here!" he yelled at me. I just looked at him. "You say that to all of your clients," I answered. Actually, the bear looked huge to me, but I had no experience for comparison.

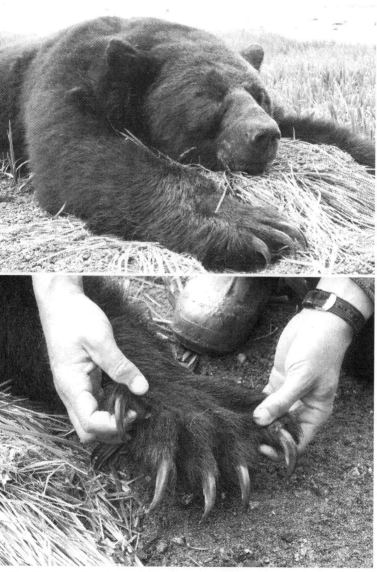

The Alaskan Black Bear was huge! His hide was perfect, although he only had one eye. His claws were as long as Brown Bear claws.

We began to examine the bear in the fading light. It had huge, long claws, more like a Brown Bear than a Black Bear. Suddenly, I looked at its right eye and it was missing! Bud went for the boat and my camera as I slowly sat down on the bear to rest and regain some strength. Its mouth was large and the teeth were an ugly green from the stain of the grass. Two teeth were missing at the gum line and the molars were worn down. He also had decay in some of the teeth. He would have been a dentist's delight. He was old! The Game & Fish Department later determined his age to be 17 years.

By the time Bud returned to the boat, the tide was moving out rapidly and he anchored the boat out even further. He brought our cameras. I took mine out and proceeded to use a flash. The batteries were dead! I had forgotten to replace them after shooting so many photos the past few days.

Bud took a couple of flash photos. I suggested that we leave the bear and return in the morning for photos. Besides I didn't want Bud skinning the bear by flashlight and making mistakes. He agreed. We spread the bear out, tagged him and returned to the boat. The long trip back to the main boat was pleasant. I seemed to glow with success. It appears that goals in life that are difficult or laborious are most appreciated. The stalk was awesome. While Bud was retrieving the boat, I paced the distance for the shot and it measured 151 yards. A reasonable distance.

The Exodus:

Our dinner after the hunt was one of celebration. The problem was that it lasted until 1:00 a.m. and by then I was so tired I didn't know my own name. I barely had energy to climb into my cherished upper bunk.

By 8:00 a.m. the next morning, we were ready to retrieve Crab pots and to skin and prepare the bear for shipping. However, we had to take time to quickly charge a battery on a nearby anchored Crab boat. After this, I changed batteries in my camera and we took all of the necessary tools and equipment and headed to the end of the bay.

The bear was undisturbed, much to my relief. I was concerned that another bear or, perhaps, a roving Wolf would ruin the hide. He looked bigger than he did the night before. I realized this when I had to help skin him and rigor mortis had stiffened the old guy up.

We moved him around for some photos. We took whole bear shots, feet, head and anything else that looked interesting. Bud is a good skinner and he made short work of the animal. He left the head and feet to be finished back at the other boat. We examined the body and found only one bullet entrance and one exit. I was surprised that the .375 H&H Magnum had gone completely through the shoulder and out the neck. Apparently since I was lying down, the bullet went through his body at an angle. Bud shot as the animal was dropping and missed him.

The Dept. of Fish and Game requires that hunters retrieve the edible portions of animals killed, including bear. However, apparently only in certain months, which makes no sense to me. But we had to take the front and back quarters out to the boat, as well as the heavy hide. I helped as best that I could, It took several rest stops for me but Bud could heft whatever and hike to the boat with ease … oh, the strength of youth!

Since today was Friday and Monday was Memorial Day, we decided to go into Petersburg and have the bear sealed by the proper authorities and then I could take it home with me as luggage. Bud would send the skull to a special company that has imported some species of beetle that would totally clean the skull without boiling. They must be special beetles since the cost is $175.

It took an hour to travel to Petersburg. I had fished out of the port in the early 1990s but had never been back. It is a charming little seaport, which also serves as a tourist trap for the large cruise ships that stop on their way up the inland canal.

We carried the bear up to a second floor laboratory room of the Game & Fish Dept. Headquarters. A pleasant woman began her routine examination of our paperwork that Bud had previously completed. And then the questions began, which I tried to answer honestly and correctly. She commented that the bear was huge, old and unusual. She didn't measure the skin since it shrinks immediately after death. Her skull measurement was 19 6/16, but we measured it to be 19 13/16. Could the skull have shrunk 7/16 in 20 hours?

About this time an Alaska State Trooper came down and began to interrogate us further on other issues. I could have re-enlisted in the military in less time and with fewer questions. Bud sealed the bear and then the woman sealed the seal and sealed the skull and then the Trooper checked the sealer's work.

We retuned by early evening and fished from the main boat until dark, without success. Several other boats had entered the sheltered bay for protection from the pending storm. That night we had the remaining Crab for dinner but we also had a Dolly that I had caught and the Halibut, but we chose Crab since we had been keeping them alive. They were so large that I could only eat one half, but Bud could eat my other half and his own. How that man could eat!

The next morning I awoke at 5:30 a.m. and realized that the trip was over. I looked out my port hole and then the window and realized that I would never see this bay or be in this boat again. My experiences with Bud and others on the trip would be singular events, like ships passing in the night, never to be seen again. I was beginning to be depressed until I looked out at the cooler containing my 8' 1 ½" trophy Black Bear and my 19 13/16" skull. I soon recovered.

Bud was exhausted and I was more tired that he. I had packed all gear on the way in. We unloaded everything, delivered the bear meat to the meat plant and he dropped me off at my motel. I placed the whole cooler in the deep freeze in preparation for taking it home on Monday.

After a hot soak of my weary bones and a nap, I arose, walked to the nearest restaurant and returned for an evening of relaxation. It was lonely, but a pleasant change to be by myself. At times, I'm not bad company.

Extended hunting and fishing trips are broad, often complicated in nature and include many enjoyable amenities not recognized by those who don't appreciate the harvesting of game. This trip, to me, will remain one of the most outstanding of my lifetime. I have hunted and fished on four continents, 11 lower states and Alaska. Killing a world class Black Bear is a once-in-a-lifetime-experience for me. How I appreciate my American citizenship, which has provided these opportunities.

The Last of a Species?

Stalking the Scimitar Oryx

I slowly pulled off Intersection #420, on Interstate #10, 20 miles east of Sonora, Texas. I had been driving for 2½ days, from Vernal, Utah. My guide and outfitter, Jason Schwarz, of the Heart A ranch, was sitting in a large, white Ford 4x4 mud-covered pickup. He waved for me to follow him north on a well maintained county road.

We drove two miles and then turned west on what could barely be called a road, more of a rock strewn trail. In fact, in all of my experience, I had never seen such rock covered range. A serious year-long drought had caused the area to look even more moon-like than an area that could be seriously hunted.

We traveled another mile, crossed a dry stream bed and then came to an eight-foot high fence with a huge gate. The Heart A ranch is similar to many ranches in Texas that are high-fenced to keep predators out and cattle and game species in.

We passed the remains of old ranching activities during the past century. The remains of old gas wells and abandoned pipelines added to the uniqueness of the ride. Jason got out and waved me to the entrance of a 1950's style ranch house. A welcomed rain of the day before was evidenced by mud and standing water in places.

As I got out of my truck, I noticed five animals that I had never seen scampering away from an old barn. I looked closely and later identified the animals as Blackbuck *(Antilope cervicapra)*; a large buck and four does. The animals originally came from India. The animal had horns at least 18 inches long and was multi-colored. The does were dull beige, with no colorful markings. The animals turned out to be the ranch pets and I affectionately named the buck "Bubba." I would see him many times in the next few days.

Bubba, the Blackbuck, with two of his does in the background.
He welcomed me coming and going from the ranch.

It was mid-afternoon. We introduced ourselves. Jason asked me how the trip had gone. I replied … "well, if you don't count closed roads, bumper to bumper traffic in Colorado from returning skiers to town, a dead battery and a 50-mile tow to Roswell, New Mexico, it was fine. I'm pleased to be here." We discussed some hunting rules and expectations. Jason then asked: "would you like to drive around and look the place over tonight and then begin hunting in the morning?" I agreed. I unpacked all of my gear, changed clothes, retrieved my binoculars and was ready to go.

The hunting vehicle was a 1995 Chevrolet Suburban, a favorite vehicle for hunting around the country. As we climbed a rocky ridge, in an easterly direction, I noticed vast numbers of dead cedars *(Juniper)* and Jason told me the drought had killed cedars all over west Texas and he feared for the hardwood trees. I then noticed that the Pin Oaks and Live Oaks were completely bare. Later, I would notice that many had buds. If more rain comes, most of the oaks will survive.

I had traveled the vast distance from home to hunt the Scimitar Oryx *(Oryx dammah)* of North Africa, now listed as probably extinct in the wild. However, large numbers exist in Texas and South Africa. The U.S. government has restricted importing them. But domestic hunting is still allowed. In April of 2012, new restrictive measures go into effect for hunting and raising them.

Instead of protecting the animals, these foolish measures will cause there to be fewer animals, especially in the U.S. Several ranchers that I visited with will not tolerate government regulations and will simply eliminate their herds. Few politicians and most of the public fail to understand that hunters have saved wildlife species around the world, especially in Africa. Since wildlife has great monetary value, it will be protected.

There are three species of Oryx and a sub-species. I have known about the Gemsbuck *(Oryx gazelle)* but I didn't get a chance to hunt them in Africa. The Arabian Oryx *(Oryx leucoryx)* is extinct, except for a few in zoos around the world. There is a sub-species of the Gemsbuck, the Fringe-eared Oryx *(Oryx beisa callotis)*. The most prominent is the Gemsbuck and is a popular game animal. There are large numbers of the Gemsbuck in the White Sands area of New Mexico, and on game ranches in Texas and South Africa.

After learning about the Scimitar, I began to be intrigued and started a search to find a location in Texas to hunt them. After a long search and visiting with different ranchers, I selected the Heart A ranch.

The Suburban slowly crawled over the large rocks and we made a Northerly turn. Now, on a high ridge, I could see the vast terrain, called the "hill country" in Texas. I soon saw flashes of Whitetail Deer *(Odocoileus virginianus)* as they scampered several hundred yards from us. Then, nearing a windmill watering trough, we saw 2 herds of Blackbuck, with smaller bucks, does and fawns disappearing into the brush.

Memories of Africa:

As we turned west and the road got worse, a few head of Axis Deer *(Cervus axis)* watched us; then two large chocolate Fallow Deer *(Dama dama)* stood hiding in the brush. I was interested in hunting a Blackbuck and an Axis Deer. However, since Axis Deer drop their antlers early, and breed all year, none could be hunted. Later we saw an axis doe with a tiny, new-born fawn. Since the ranch had several water sources the wildlife appeared to be well distributed.

As we crawled along, memories came back of my hunting in Arica. It was very similar; never knowing what animals would be seen, some animals more alert than others, some animals fleeing from long distances; a surprise around every curve.

We soon came upon three Buffalo (*Bison bison*). The extreme drought had made them lose their caution as we approached. A few minutes later we jumped a large herd of Elk (*Cervus canadensis*), more cautious than the Buffalo caused by needing supplemental feed. Jason noted than there were large bulls that refused to be seen in spite of their need for feed. They apparently had become almost totally nocturnal.

Jason said that there were a few Sika Deer *(Cervus nippon)* on the ranch but they are so wary that they have also become mostly nocturnal. They have been seen very few times and would be very difficult to hunt. In this part of the hill country there are significant numbers of free-ranging Axis and Sika Deer and they can be hunted on the private land.

We were now slowly moving toward the far northwest corner of the ranch. There was a large windmill, with watering troughs for the animals. As we approached, Jason excitingly said: "look at the Turkeys." Sure enough Turkeys were everywhere, scurrying from the troughs in several directions. I have hunted Turkeys but not in the south. Texas Turkeys are known as Rio Grande. The western Turkeys are Merriam, a sub-species, but both known as (*Meleagris gallapavo).*

We were so busy watching the Turkeys that we almost missed a small herd of Scimitars moving south away from us. They were all cows and calves. One old cow had huge horns. She could have been 15 years old, Jason said. Those horns were probably longer than any of the bulls. It was easy to see that she was pregnant. The beautiful animals didn't appear too frightened but they silently moved into dense cover. The Scimitars looked just like the many photos I had viewed over the past year. They were large, mostly white, with beige-brown markings on their necks and faces.

Jason said that there were two herds of Scimitars. The other larger herd had more cows and calves, a large herd bull and some smaller bulls. He then informed me that we would try to find a single bull that had been separated from the others for several years. "The critter refuses to be social!" I asked: "which bull is the largest?" Jason said that he thought the loner would be larger but he couldn't be sure since he had never seen them together.

So, our plans were set for tomorrow. I suddenly became excited! We would try to find the lone bull; if not we would try to find the other herd and take the herd bull, which ever came first.

We traveled a different road back to the ranch. We saw several Whitetail bucks as they raised their tail flags and scampered off. Whitetail Deer are the smartest of all deer, in my opinion. The drought had not changed their behavior where they could acquire water. We slowly descended the rocky ridge to the ranch. As we approached the out buildings, there was Bubba to welcome us home.

By now, I was totally exhausted. I removed my binoculars, jacket, boots and crawled upon the bed to rest until dinner. Since I was the only guest at the ranch, Jason cooked and we ate together in the comfortable trophy room.

The temperature was forecasted to be in the low 20's. Jason said that he would have to shut off all of the water since the pump and pipes were not winterized and could freeze and break. The weather had appeared to be balmy to me since I had been living in temperatures nearing zero for weeks. I wasn't even wearing gloves. Hopefully, my bodily functions would be coordinated with the condition of the plumbing until morning.

The morning dawned clear, bright, without a cloud in the sky. It was cold. Frost and ice had formed on everything in sight. The water was turned on and everything appeared fine … especially after a good breakfast of eggs, sausage and Jason's mother's homemade bread, sent over, especially for me.

This was the day! Jason started the old Suburban and left it warming while I packed the necessary gear for the morning. I had wanted to use a Winchester Lever Action .405, the exact gun that President Theodore Roosevelt had used in Africa. However, after thinking about the probable distance, using open sights, I opted for my old, common, experienced Ruger Model 77 .30-06. Picking up that gun was like putting on an old pair of boots or like greeting an old friend, whom I had known and felt completely comfortable around. Indeed, I had killed 22 different species of game around the world with that gun.

As we began our climb up the rocky ridge again, there was old Bubba. Yesterday he had four does; this morning he had six does. What had he been doing during the night? We topped the ridge and looked West and North. The sun was nipping at the roof of the ranch house, with a little steam rising. My binoculars were tight around my neck; my gun had four shells in the magazine; my shooting sticks were in the back and I was sipping on a bottle of water.

I mentioned to Jason that the cold night and bright day should motivate every animal to move. Jason responded: "we'll see." We had driven for several minutes across the ridge going north. Nothing was in sight. We continued on past two or three Whitetail blinds. Jason stopped the truck and I glassed west. Two Whitetail does stood watching us at 400 yards then were gone in a flash. Crawling along northeast, as we grew nearer to a waterhole, several Blackbuck does, with two smaller bucks disappeared into the brush. I wondered if Bubba had stolen two of their does.

Crawling on, we saw nothing, as we crossed two dilapidated fences. Suddenly, I saw something that flashed white directly ahead of us at about 400 yards. I told Jason; he immediately stopped and backed the Suburban back across the old fence. He moved until we could better glass the animal. At first, we thought it was a white Fallow Deer. The animal was coming in our direction!

Jason suddenly blurted out "It's that lone bull Scimitar. I haven't seen it in several weeks." "Are we that lucky?" I retorted. We were well hidden and the bull was coming our way. I quickly got out, careful not to slam the door, and grabbed my shooting sticks. Jason was close behind me. By now, the bull, moving rapidly, was within 200 yards. If the animal didn't detect us, it could come close to us. There was no wind movement. Jason pointed to a way through the brush. I pumped a shell into the barrel and tried to set up my shooting sticks.

I didn't realize how nervous I was as I clumsily set the sticks up only to have them collapse. I set them up again and looked but there was no clear path to see the animal. I set them up for the third time in a better location. The bull had slowed down, perhaps sensing us, but kept moving, now quartering from us. I could see him well. "Is he as good as the herd bull?" I asked. Jason said: "I'm not sure." Do you want to try to find the other bull?" "NO! I'll take this bull. We may never see any more."

A great Scimitar Oryx trophy. The horns were 38 inches
long and we estimated it to weigh 400 lbs.

I adjusted the sticks as the bull was now directly across from us at only 50
yards. I had made a decision, should I find the bull, that I would take a
suggestion that I had recently read in a sporting magazine to shoot more for
the heart instead of the lungs. In retrospect, I should have shot it in the neck.
The bull, sensing us, stopped for a second then began to quickly move away,
I squeezed the trigger. The shot rang out; the bull jumped straight up. I could
see the bullet hit low in the left front shoulder. It was a perfect heart shot.
"Good shot!" Jason yelled at me. The bull disappeared in a group of juniper
trees 100 yards away. I pumped another shell in the barrel, set the safety and
grabbed my shooting sticks. Jason took them from me and pointed the way
to go.

Behind the largest juniper tree, we found the bull. It was as majestic in death
as it was in life. The long tapering, saber-like horns were huge. I stood for a
minute just looking at it. Then a surge of regret overcame me, as it has many
times before, after killing a magnificent trophy animal. Death is part of life
for humans as well as animals. If animals are left without concern for adequate

food, water and cover, to multiply uncontrollably, then death will surely come and will not be as merciful as from appropriate hunting.

We took a few photos and I began to look the animal over closely. Jason ran to the Suburban and retrieved a tape measure. The sweeping horns measured 38 inches in length; a gold medal by Safari Club International standards. I stayed with the animal while Jason returned to the ranch and brought back an hydraulic trailer to take the animal to the processor.

We decided to take the animal to Ingram, Texas, a small town 80 miles east of the ranch. Texans don't measure distance in miles, they measure it in hours … so it was 1½ hours east of the ranch. The processor was also a taxidermist. However, I decided to bring the horns and cape back to Vernal and have my own taxidermist mount it. The meat would be ready by Friday so that gave me another day to enjoy viewing the animals and photographing them.

We met Jason's father, Elgin, co-owner of the ranch in Ingram. Jason treated us both to lunch and the three of us returned to the ranch. The evening was enjoyable as we talked about old hunts, old cars, old guns and old people. Old people usually talk about the past since they don't have much future.

The next day was spent in hiking, resting and in making two more trips across the ranch. We never did see the Scimitar herd and so I'll never know which bull was the largest.

On Friday, I bid goodbye to Jason and Elgin. I thanked them both for their hospitality and wished them well in the future of their ranch. Leaving people and hunting areas is sometimes emotional for me. This is especially true when I know there is little likelihood of ever seeing them again. As we moved away from the ranch house, there was Bubba. He appeared to be more interested in his harem that he was in watching me leave.

SECTION IV – POLITICS

●

A few opinions on the
Constitution,
some war stories,
cars, trucks
and whatever

The Politics of Bravery

Fire on the Hangar Deck

*(**NOTE**: Recent and past publications describing the conflagration that occurred on August 6, 1952, on the USS BOXER, off North Korea, have been general in nature and more detailed information is apparently unknown. This first-person description might be of interest to historians and to the reader).*

In January, 1952, I was stationed in a medical dispensary at the naval boot camp in Bainbridge, Maryland. I was ordered to report to San Francisco to meet the USS BOXER and join the ship's company of corpsmen.

I reported aboard ship the first of February as an HM3; later I was promoted to HM2 before leaving the ship. We arrived in Yokosuka, Japan in March. We operated in Task Force 77, with three other carriers and support ships.

At the time of the accident we were operating off North Korea. The morning of August 6, I had the duty in sick bay. I was the only one awake when general quarters sounded. My station for general quarters was at the forward end of the hangar deck, with a crew of firefighters.

I grabbed my first aid equipment and climbed up to the hangar deck aft and started down the deck. The whole hangar deck was covered with planes, loaded and awaiting transfer to the flight deck, for the next flight assignment. The smoke was intense and I could hear .50 caliber shells bouncing off the bulkheads. I continued forward until I was nearer the planes. The smoke was now intense and the sound of exploding shells was deafening to me.

I knew that I shouldn't go forward on the hangar deck. I went aft and down two decks and then went forward. By now the smoke had drifted to the lower decks. I attempted to go through several bunking compartments but the crews were waking up and the chaos prevented me from going forward. Most of the men were still half asleep and didn't know what was going on. The smoke was acrid. I took pillow cases and showed a few men to wet them and put them over their mouths and noses to improve their breathing.

I realized I couldn't get to my assigned position, so I went topside to the flight deck. There I found some sailors coming from below with burns and choking from the smoke. I continued to assist those that I could and stayed in the general area of the flight deck. I didn't feel safe in going below again. I never saw any of my superiors for direction.

There wasn't much activity on the flight deck, since all of the planes and fire were on the hangar deck. The flight crews were scuttling all planes and equipment over the side. The ballast was shifted to cause the ship to list heavily starboard to make it easier for the crews. Seeing such a large ship listing was frightening to me.

After about an hour, the order was sounded to prepare to abandon ship. By now a few men were jumping off the decks; I didn't give that a second thought. I didn't know what "prepare to abandon ship meant," since I had never heard such a command before. I continued to treat those that I could with what meager supplies that I had.

Burns are terribly painful and intense heat makes the skin flaccid and liquid-like over the exposed areas. I gave what morphine I had to those in need. I continued to remain in the same general area.

The other support ships had now come closer but there wasn't anything that they could do. The fate of the ship remained with those fighting the fire and removing the loaded planes and debris. Fortunately, no bombs exploded, for if any had, the ship would have surely been lost.

After about two hours, the order was given to stand down from the abandon ship command. By afternoon, the fire was suppressed and things became more normal. I returned to the sick bay where many wounded were being treated. I never saw any other corpsmen during the whole time. And, of course, I never did get to my assigned position on the forward hangar deck.

Eight men were killed. Three of the eight were two corpsmen and one doctor. All three were assigned to the plane squadrons and were not part of ship's company. They were assigned to the 02 decks for sleeping. Those decks were located over the hangar deck. The intense flames and heat expanded hatch frames. The hatches could not be opened and all three died, unable to escape.

I don't recall the numbers of wounded, although they were not as many as might be expected. Since we were too far at sea to send the bodies back, they were stored in the food refrigeration compartments until we returned to Japan.

We limped back to Yokosuka and anchored out. Japanese repairmen did temporary repairs and then we returned to San Francisco and immediately were put into dry dock for further repairs. I left the ship the next spring, while still in dry dock. I was assigned to a flight squadron in San Diego, where I finished my enlistment at a family dispensary, delivering babies. From fire injuries to delivering babies!

I don't know if an official inquiry was made; I assume so. However, I never did read one. The accident was man-caused. Apparently, a member of a flight crew accidently fired a gun and the shells went into the plane forward and that started the whole affair.

A few weeks after the fire, three corpsmen, including me, were nominated for the Navy-Marine Corps Medal. It was decided that three medals were too many; only one would be awarded. It was given to our unit commander, a man by the name of I.P. Irons, a full Commander and M.D. It was awarded for burning his hand on a hot handrail. Strangely, none of the enlisted personnel saw him anywhere during the fire.

I *was* given a commendation:

From: Commanding Officer
To: Mahaffey, Benjamin D., 388 15 14 HM3, USN

Subject: Letter of Commendation

1. During a major fire aboard this vessel on 6 August, 1952, while operating against North Korean and Chinese Communist forces,

despite smoke and heat you made your way to your fire station and displayed outstanding courage without regard for your personal safety in making repeated trips into the raging inferno and into smoke filled compartments to evacuate asphyxiated personnel and wounded. Your personal courage and professional skill in caring for wounded enabled you to save many shipmates' lives and to reduce materially the number of casualties. Your zealous devotion to duty in the face of extreme personal peril was in keeping with the highest traditions of the United States Naval Service.

2. It is with a great deal of pleasure that I commend you for your outstanding service.

3. A copy of this letter will be made a part of your service record.

M.B. GURNEY
Captain, USS BOXER

I have no idea who wrote the letter or who nominated me. It was inaccurate, of course, in most ways. I knew nothing about it. It just appeared in the mail one day. The real heroes were the fire fighting crews, and I doubt that few, if any of them, received the recognition so justly due. It appears that few people, if any, understand the politics of bravery.

Is anybody there? Does anybody care?

The Shredding of the Constitution

It was the summer of 1776. Continental Congress was in session. Delegates from the 13 colonies were trying to agree on language declaring independence from England and the formation of a new nation.

The colonies were already at war with England. George Washington was the commanding general of what was loosely called the Continental Army.

The army was in terrible condition. Washington wrote regular letters to the Congress, notifying and requesting assistance, most of which were unanswered. Finally, out of desperation, in one letter, he expounded "Is anybody there? Does anybody care?"

That plea is relevant today in regards to the massive government intervention in our lives and the shredding of the Constitution. What is the Constitution? It is the founding document, with the philosophy of governance and the bylaws for administering our government.

A most important declaration is that this nation is a Constitutional Republic, not a democracy, as most people believe. Our individual rights come from God and not some mortal or man-contrived organization. The word democracy is not mentioned in any of the founding documents.

This founding principle is important. The rights of the minority must be protected. An example of democracy or mobocracy, is a lynch mob; the majority rules. The only dissenter is at the end of the rope.

Later, in 1798, Thomas Jefferson, in a paper discussing the power of government and its servants stated: *"In question of power, then, let no more be heard of confidence in man, but bind him down from mischief by the chains of the Constitution."*

Today, not only are the chains of the Constitution loosened, but many links are missing. Restoration of founding principles will be difficult, but we should not be condemned for not trying.

General Provisions:

Space does not permit a lengthy discussion of the general provisions. However, a note should be given to the general philosophy of the founding fathers. The introduction or preamble:

"We the people of the United States, in order to form a more perfect union, establish justice, ensure domestic tranquility, provide for the common defense, promote the general welfare, and secure the blessings of liberty to ourselves and our posterity, do ordain and establish the Constitution for the United States of America."

Benjamin Franklin: *" ... from such an assembly (delegates) can a perfect production be expected? It therefore astonishes me, sir to find such a system approaching so near to perfection as it does."*

Franklin also said: *"Our new Constitution is now established, and has an appearance that promises permanency; but in this world nothing can be said to be certain, except death and taxes."*

Today, the "we the people" clause, defined at that time, seems unbelievable. White males who didn't own property, women and blacks were not included. However, the framers knew that amendments would be necessary, and those above weaknesses have been solved.

The Constitution is not a living document, but neither has rigor mortis paralyzed it. Changes, when necessary, are long and difficult, which protects the original intent and causes great debate and interest. A recent example is the Equal Rights Amendment. After years of debate and effort, the amendment barely failed passage.

Although the founding fathers were brilliant, George Washington wrote in

1787: *"I do not think we are more inspired, have more wisdom, or possess more virtue, than those who will come after us."* But Washington was not aware of the great moral decay that would sweep the nation 200 years later.

Why has our Republic degraded to its present condition? Why have our leaders failed us? Why won't our leaders uphold the Constitution? Why do the majority not represent us? Why do they experiment with our future by dissolving our sovereignty? Why are we evolving into a nanny state?

Frosty Wooldridge has written that a Constitutional Republic requires four standards:

(1) It demands a highly educated population that thinks critically and is aware and participates in the affairs of the nation at all levels.

(2) It requires citizens to have a similar moral code, regardless of various religions.

(3) It insists on a mutual ethical system abided by all.

(4) It must have a single language, whereby all citizens can discuss, debate, adopt resolutions and initiate mutual beneficial action for society as a whole.

If the above conditions are true, our nation is seriously failing on all of them, and our failures are easily answered.

In the original Articles, there were no term limits set for legislators or the President. This was, perhaps, the most serious mistake in the document. President Franklin Roosevelt was elected to four terms. This frightened some and so Amendment XXII limited the president to two terms of four years. But no terms have been established for our legislators.

Perhaps, the single greatest threat to our Constitution and the nation is the career politicians who are supposed to represent us. In the last 30 years, American apathy has risen and Congressional ethics have fallen. Voters return inept, corrupt and marginalized politicians back into office term after term. Legislators try to serve into their 80's and 90's.

An apparent false assumption made by the founders was that legislators were citizens first and politicians second. They would serve a term or two and return to their former professions. Little did they realize how the media attention, salaries, benefits, trappings and power would intoxicate almost all who are elected, addict them and render them impotent to the real purpose of serving.

The Constitution divides the governance into three parts, all supposing to provide checks and balances to each other. These lines are becoming more vague and controversial. The courts are legislating from the bench and attempting to change societal norms. The legislature is abrogating its responsibility to the President in declaring war. The last three wars were never declared by Congress.

Then, Congress tries to influence the conducting of the wars by manipulating financial support. If Congress won't agree with some of the President's agenda, he tries to use Executive orders to get around approval. Almost all of the legislative bills that are passed have scores of amendments, with appropriations that will benefit individual legislators in their home districts, helping to insure their re-election.

A recent example is the 2008 $700B bailout called the Emergency Economic Stabilization Act (EESA). According to George Will, Congress didn't make a law. Rather, it made the Executive Branch into legislators. It gave the President broad powers to spend vast amounts of money without specific enough guidelines.

According to the logic of the Constitution in the separation of powers, limits are implied in the kind of discretion that Congress may confer on the Executive Branch.

The Supreme Court has said: "That Congress cannot delegate legislative power to the President is a principle universally recognized as vital to the integrity and maintenance of the system of government ordained by the Constitution."

And the Court has said that properly delegated discretion must come with "an intelligible principle" and must "clearly delineate" a policy that limits the discretion. EESA fails that test. This is just one example. The present administration is moving so rapidly in an anti-Constitution direction, that many other examples, especially in the socialization of the banks, auto industry and lending institutions could be illustrated. Should our President be running General Motors?

The Assault on the Bill of Rights:

The Constitution, as now written, could not be accepted by many Constitutional Convention delegates. These wise men, Christians, historians, and legal scholars realized that the citizens needed to be protected *from* the government. Therefore the first ten amendments were called the Bill of Rights.

These men were inspired as well as wise; citizens need to be protected from the government. The history of past systems of government show all forms of government eventually became corrupt, failed and suppressed the people for whom they were established to serve and protect.

More than 11,000 Constitutional Amendments have been introduced in Congress since 1789. Of these, only 33 received the necessary two thirds vote and were submitted to the states for ratification. Six of those have never been ratified.

There have only been 27 amendments to the Constitution, but there have been scores of violations of the Constitution, most of which have gone unnoticed by the populace and scorned by our representatives. Each legislator and President swears to uphold and defend the Constitution but few take their oath seriously. Many legislators have probably never read the full document.

Actually, there have only been 25 amendments since the 18th Amendment concerning prohibition was repealed by the 21st amendment. The amendments to the Constitution are much better known and exposed than the general operational provisions of the document. These amendments appear to affect the people more directly, but be not fooled, all aspects of the Constitution are important to each citizen's freedoms.

The amendments are not listed in the order of importance. In the original version of the Bill of Rights, the current first amendment was listed third. Many believe that the 2nd Amendment protecting the right to bear arms is the most important since it guarantees all of the other amendments.

The following are a few brief examples of the assault on selected amendments:

Amendment I: *Congress shall make no law respecting an establishment of religion or prohibiting the free exercise thereof; or abridging the freedom of speech or of the press; or the right of the people peaceably to assemble and to petition the Government for redress of grievances.*

This amendment is designed to protect four freedoms but is constantly being eroded. Freedom of speech and freedom of religion are closely associated. Pornography is protected but the Ten Commandments are constantly being removed from the public arena. Prayers in schools and public places are assaulted as a violation of the church and state association.

Intelligent design, otherwise known as creationism, has been removed from our schools along with prayer. A simple review of the amendment reveals the above examples are a bizarre interpretation.

President Obama, during a recent foreign visit, declared that America is not a Christian nation. The framers were Christians and most of the clauses are based on Christian principles. There are literally thousands of references to deity, divine providence and many other terms in their writings. The fact that we get our rights from God is a Christian principle.

Many aspects of the press are not free. The major media is controlled by powerful men and corporations who have agendas and their reporting reflects their views. This is dangerous since most Americans are poorly read, study little and are motivated by short sound bites delivered by convincing people.

Surprisingly the assembly clause is changing. In urban areas, to meet, to protest or to rally requires permits, often requires limitations of various kinds, i.e., physical distances, etc.

The redress clause appears to, generally, be intact, if you have enough money to hire lawyers and to successfully get on a court docket. Here, we find judges are often inept and know little about the constitution. It appears that a citizen can get as much justice as he can afford.

Amendment II: *A well regulated militia, being necessary to the security of a free state, the right of the people to keep and bear arms, shall not be infringed.*

The false philosophy that "guns kill people," instead of "people kill people" causes a constant battle over this freedom. Various levels of government are constantly passing or trying to pass laws to prohibit the private ownership of guns. It would appear that the statement "the right of the people to keep and bear arms" would be clear enough.

Various strategies are used to circumvent the Constitution. Banning what is termed assault weapons was tried. The definition was made as broad as possible to include some sporting weapons. The law was passed but later rescinded by a time clause. The attempt to pass another similar ban is surely coming. Back door methods are constantly in committee, i.e., excessive taxation, banning certain types of bullets, holding gun manufacturers responsible for the use of manufactured weapons, etc.

America is becoming more violent but controlling firearms will not change the deteriorating nature of man. Some gains in defending this right have been made. Concealed firearms permits are being offered in more states. The handgun ban in Washington, D.C. was over turned by the Supreme Court. As a result, many cities and counties have to revise their local laws.

The gun lobby is one of the strongest in Congress and has been mostly successful in the defense of the Second Amendment. This amendment will remain one of the most important and controversial in all of the Constitution.

Amendment X: *The powers not delegated to the United States by the Constitution, nor prohibited by it to the States, are reserved to the States respectively, or to the people.*

The other original amendments in the Bill of Rights all refer, in some way, to the rights of individuals. But the Tenth Amendment protects powers, not rights ... to the states ... and not to individuals. The struggle between federalism and states' rights has been ongoing since the beginning of the nation. This single issue was the major cause of the Civil War.

As of this writing, this Amendment is the center of several major breaches in the Constitution. One issue is the Obama Health Care Bill and the other is the issue of enforcement of illegal immigration. The Supreme Court is to rule on the Health Care Bill during this session. The Federal Government is suing several states that are trying to protect their borders and control illegal immigration.

For decades, the Tenth Amendment has been ignored and the Federal Government has continued to broaden its powers over the sovereignty of the states. Ignoring the Amendment, the Federal Government has created a monstrous system of entitlements, many forced on the States. As a result, the national and state debts are unsustainable. The current national debt is over fifteen trillion dollars and most states are technically bankrupt. It will be interesting, but probably catastrophic in the manner this will work.

Amendment XIV: <u>Section 1:</u> *All persons born or naturalized in the United States and subject to the jurisdiction thereof, are citizens of the United States and of the State wherein they reside. No State shall make or enforce any law which shall abridge the privileges or immunities of citizens of the United States; nor shall any State deprive any person of life, liberty, or property, without due process of law; nor deny to any person within its jurisdiction the equal protection of the laws.*

There are five sections in this amendment. Just the first section will be discussed. The fourteenth amendment specifically addressed the states, thereby expanding the reach of the U.S. Constitution. As a result, the Fourteenth Amendment is cited more in litigation than any other. Often, the First Amendment and the Fourteenth Amendment are used together in litigation.

The gay rights issue is currently a major point of discussion, in regards to individual rights. Should gays have equal protection to be able to marry or to re-define the definition of marriage? Are they protected in the general welfare clauses; or the pursuit of happiness clause?

If the Supreme Court should rule in their favor, can the Fourteenth Amendment protect those who want to practice polygamy or polyandry? Can a person marry an animal using this argument? This amendment is being assaulted or stretched to near its breaking point in logic.

Equal protection in the administration of laws and justice is a core right in this Republic. This amendment has been used to right injustice for thousands of people. It has been used in the workplace, in corporations, in the government, etc.

This amendment was used to protect blacks after the Civil War to define the legal status of slaves. In was instrumental in breaking "Black Codes" designed to restrict the lives of newly freed slaves. Now, all citizens are protected by its clauses … if a citizen is aware of them and pursues justice.

<u>There is reason for hope:</u>

The assault on our individual rights will never end. However, there is hope that an educated population can stem the tide and eventually reverse the losing of our rights.

To be successful we must educate ourselves and those around us of the dangers we face. We must return to the Judeo-Christian moral and ethical code. We must stop illegal immigration where we are allowing vast numbers of people to enter this nation and establish large social enclaves, speaking a foreign language at the expense of English, our official language.

Here's a suggestion for you. A great, simple, logical guide to the Constitution is ***THE WORDS WE LIVE BY,*** a wonderful book, by Linda Monk, published by Stonesong Press. It can be purchased on the internet at a modest price.

AN ODE TO
THE PRESIDENT

There once was a man named Obama,
Who wounded the nation with trauma.
He's young and naïve, and seeks to deceive.
Is that what he learned from his mama?

His appointees are lax and never pay tax,
But to Democrats, it doesn't matter.
They're the ones that we need,
In spite of their greed, over any logical chatter.

He'll bring us some change,
Though to some it seems strange,
To spend into total oblivion.
He'll increase our tax and none
Can relax in a nation that's great to live in.

But don't be depressed, we'll all do our best
To end his reign of stark terror.
In 2012 we'll have elections again
And change this nation forever.

In Defense of Clara Stringham*

NOTE:

Clara Stringham is a young woman who joined the Navy from Vernal, Utah. While serving, several experiences caused her to question the wisdom of changing the "don't ask; don't tell" policy of the armed forces concerning gays serving openly in the military. She wrote a letter to the VERNAL EXPRESS concerning her opinions. She was viciously attacked from several responses to the letter. This is my letter to the editor in her defense.

Congratulations, Clara Stringham. You expressed your opinion of the "Don't Ask; Don't Tell" policy of the military and were viciously attacked, personally, by a half page of sniping ranters from the anonymous protection of the internet.

Clara, you are correct in your statements. At worst, the policy should be continued; at best, homosexuals should be denied from serving in the military. Although they are as talented or more talented as others, they are not needed in the military. In a nation of 310 million, our military can do without them.

If we allow gays to serve openly, what about transgender and cross dressing gays? I can see it now. A person enlists in the military as a gay cross dresser. When being issued uniforms (s)he gets a male and a female uniform and then, each day, has the privilege of being what gender (s)he wants to be!

All of her/his commissioned and non-commissioned officers will be sent to "Gay Cross Dressing Sensitivity Training." (S)he will be allotted two locker spaces since (s)he will have two wardrobes. (S)he will be given unisex bathroom facilities. On days of roll call, (s)he will be given extra time to put on makeup and straighten his/her panty hose.

Why, it's only fair! How can we deny anyone his/her rights? *Homosexuality is not a question of civil rights; it's a question or morality.*

In November, 1950, after Navy medical corpsman training, I was shipped to a large Naval hospital on St. Albans, Long Island, New York. The Korean War was raging as our army was being driven to the sea. Casualties were great and many wounded army veterans were treated there.

Corpsmen were scarce and we worked 16 hour days. As a result, a Reserve Navy Medical Corpsman Unit had been activated. Many members were gay and knew each other. I was billeted in a room with at least one homosexual. I had to remove him from my bed the second night.

Gay men change their behavior when they are together or when they feel free to behave in ways that they like. As long as they are few in number or unknown they act as other men. The numbers of gays were such that they began to influence who would work with whom and who would be billeted with whom, etc. They began to form groups of five to seven here and there. Their behavior soon began to affect the operation of the hospital.

The Office of Naval Intelligence (precursor to the CIA) was called in for a full investigation. Interviews were conducted and many were immediately discharged. I was caught in the web since I was a youngster and didn't appear very masculine. I passed the investigation and went on to serve aboard a warship in Korea and had a safe, successful enlistment.

This pseudo, false, liberal acceptance of any and all behavior in society is part of a larger problem. Does anyone know of a nation or culture in the history of this planet that survived by having mercenary women, single, married, etc. and homosexuals defend itself? At the same time, millions of able-bodied men in their twenties and thirties who are still living at home or who are unemployed refuse to serve.

I've been associated with many gays in my lifetime, mostly professional. I never had any problem with them ... except in the military. My brother was homosexual. I watched, with sadness, his life unfold a chapter at a time for seventy years. He finally died an agonizing death as a result of his lifestyle and habits. Has the public forgotten that the dangerous behavior of gay men was a major contributing factor in the AIDS epidemic?

I resent the gay lobby for high jacking a perfectly good English word, never to be the same again. The word is a misnomer. The life is not gay for long. Most old gay men are usually sad, lonely and abandoned by their many partners of the past, as they age and grow unattractive. There appears to be no natural, spiritual or social affinity for long term relationships.

Although difficult to imagine in Vernal, Utah, in other areas, homosexuality is a large and growing sub-culture. We have gay: communities, bars, restaurants, TV, books, magazines, web sites and DVDs. Further, if gay marriage is adopted nationally, the action will weaken the institution of marriage forever. Then, under the equal protection clause of the 14th Amendment, polygamy, polyandry and who knows what will come next. A person will eventually be able to have a relation with a goat and call it a marriage!

As Christians, we should condemn the aberrant behavior of homosexuals. We can love the person but hate the actions. Scriptures condemn it; logic tells us that we should not let the powerful national gay lobby negatively affect our nation. Remember, rampant homosexual behavior was one factor for the fall of the Roman Empire.

Clara, be careful in declaring your feelings about homosexuals. Truth will not protect you; only conformance to what is the imposed philosophic whim of the day.

BEN D. MAHAFFEY
Vernal, Utah

Name changed for obvious reasons

Don't Mourn For Me

Occasionally, a famous person is interviewed in print or on TV about his life. Many, when asked if he would change anything in his live, if he could live it over again, reply: "I wouldn't change a thing!" How arrogant to think, in retrospect, one is satisfied with all of his life's decisions!

I, on the other hand, would change many of my decisions. Most would be centered on the way that I associated with people. However, if I could return, I *might* make many different decisions that have been life changing. Perhaps, these different "roads taken" would be *less* successful than the ones I did take, but my motivation would be to improve upon my Christian behavior.

When I review the changes that I have seen, in all aspects of life, it becomes almost unbelievable. When I was a child in a one-room school, we didn't even have ballpoint pens; they hadn't been invented! Nor had television, micro-wave ovens, computers, calculators, cell phones, blackberries, iphones, Kindles, Nooks, digital cameras, jet planes and our marvelous cars and trucks. Face book in those days meant, literally, your face was in a book, intently reading.

On the other hand, our morality, manners, and consideration for others have not kept up with technology. The last two generations could match or beat any other hedonistic group in the history of the world! We are viewing a massive, sweeping wave of immorality, graft, greed and corruption on every side. The older generations know this but the younger generations appear to be clueless. This is mostly caused by a lack of any knowledge of history, economics, social science or religion.

The concept of the "American Dream" is unknown to the latter generations. This dream has been described as knowing that with righteous ambition, work and education, any person can rise and become whatever he wants to be … in America. There are some, of course, who know this and are on track for such success, but not many.

We are rearing a generation that can be described as the "entitlement generation." This attitude means that just by *being* a being, we deserve and are endowed with whatever it is that we want with no work, effort or logic for receiving it. If this is accurate, then each succeeding generation will become worse.

Is the American Dream still alive? Perhaps, to some. However, the government cannot provide the benefits that individuals deem their birthright, anymore than can something be created out of nothing. For a free benefit to one person means that benefit was taken from another. The government cannot create anything.

I have been privileged to live the American Dream. This dream is more than becoming wealthy; for I am not wealthy. It encompasses the feeling that I have been successful, based on hard work, education, control and discipline. I have been able to have great personal freedom and to obtain the resources to support my family in a reasonable lifestyle. I have been able to see part of the world and pursue my passions and I have done so with great appreciation.

My two brothers and I were orphaned in 1937. I was adopted by my father's brother; my middle brother, Charles, was adopted by my mother's sister. No one was interested in my oldest brother, Ray, and so he was shuffled from home to home until he went on the streets and took care of himself.

Ray served in Army artillery, in the Pacific Theater, during WWII. Charles served in the Navy toward the end of WWII and during the Korean War. I served as a Navy Medic during the Korean War. Charles and I served at the same time but never together and, in fact, we never met during the war.

Emotional problems caused Ray to adapt a destructive life style and never did recover from his mental issues. Charles worked hard and obtained a middle class status. Ray and Charles didn't like each other; but both appeared to tolerate me. I don't recall the three of us being together as adults. I did associate with Charles in the 1960's and Ray in the 1980's. But none of us appeared to be close as brothers should be.

My home, although loveless, was a protective environment for my behavior. Fear of punishment appears to be an effective deterrent to foolish actions. I am grateful to have been kept in school until I graduated from High School in 1950. Shortly after graduation I joined the Navy; a few days later, the Korean War began.

I appeared to be driven with ambition more than my brothers. I returned from the War and became an apprentice printer. I became a journeyman in 1957. Soon after, I enrolled in Casper College and went to school days and worked nights on a morning newspaper. After graduating in 1961, my family and I moved to Fort Collins, Colorado, where I enrolled at Colorado State University.

Pell Grants and other types of assistance were not available in those days and I had already used the G. I. Bill for my apprentice training. Therefore, Barbara and I had to both work to keep me in school. I commuted to Loveland, Colorado where I worked nights on a weekly newspaper. Barbara had several different secretarial jobs.

Graduating, penniless, with some debt, we moved to Sedona, Arizona where I began what was supposed to be a career in the U.S. Forest Service, on the Coconino National Forest. I had already worked summers in Colorado and was somewhat experienced in that agency.

I soon learned that I was not emotionally capable or adapted to such a bureaucracy, especially with such low wages. After four years, I resigned and we moved to College Station, Texas, where I became an Instructor and began my Master's program. This period was incredibly useful as I began the most rigorous and enjoyable period of learning and growth in my lifetime.

In 1969, I graduated, with an M.S., after eight semesters. Unable to find a job suitable to my wants, I began a Ph.D. program and continued to teach and to write. I graduated in 1972 and was hired to begin a new program in Natural Resource Management at Kansas State University, Manhattan, Kansas.

I taught and was an administrator at KSU for 12 years. Six of the 12 years were very successful, under the administration that hired me. I made great strides with the program and with my personal growth. Then the politics changed and for the next six years, I could do nothing correct in the eyes of my supervisors. I was persecuted in every possible way to motivate me to leave.

However, believing that I was correct in my behavior and in my plans for administering the academic program, I tried to defend myself, using the first and fourteenth Amendments to the Constitution. After six years of stress, and a 10 day administrative trial, I was acquitted of the charges against me and I resigned with a financial settlement.

However, because of the notoriety of the trial and the length of the litigation, my teaching career ended. No other university would hire a person so controversial. The whole issue appeared as career quicksand. But after extricating myself, I found that there would be great changes in my life. However, I and my family paid a dear price for such a long and sordid experience.

Then came a period of great growth, travel and challenge. I became a private consultant to Fortune 500 companies and the military. I spent four years as a private consultant to the Army at the Pentagon. I learned a great deal and that experience continues to be useful to me today.

Afterward, came several years in private business. I purchased a retail propane company in Randolph, Kansas. The operation of this company proved deeply challenging, yet highly profitable. In 1996 we retired to Vernal, Utah, in preparation for the opening of the Temple.

I have worked intermittently as an ordinance worker and in assisting Barbara in her genealogy work. With over 50 years of effort, we have performed ordinances for over 10,000 people. It has been a privilege and honor to assist the Father in bringing to pass the immortality and eternal life of man.

Many people have lived the American dream. But most of the time it is incomplete … without understanding the Gospel of Jesus Christ. If membership in the Church of Jesus Christ of Latter-day Saints can be added to the other opportunities, as an American, how can one fail?

I became converted to the Church in 1957. After gaining my testimony, I have never looked back. I have served in many positions in seven states across this great nation. Barbara has also contributed to my efforts, in addition to her own successful church career. My sons and grandchildren are not so inclined. Although disappointing to us, we realize that agency is the supreme law of the universe. Perhaps, some day, each son, wife, grandchild can learn the great value of membership and activity in the church.

I was born in obscurity and I will die in obscurity. But, wow, the time between has been an exciting journey. I have lived the American dream, thanks to many people who helped me. I have been a printer, writer, forest ranger, college professor, private businessman, and consultant.

I've had the pleasure to pursue my passions: travel, photography, gardening, fishing, hunting, history, and politics. I've traveled some of the world; hunted and fished on four continents. And still, I received my beginning in a small town in the middle of the wilderness of Wyoming.

Have I made mistakes? Many. Would I correct them? Yes. However, I might not do any better the second time around. I have learned that life is nothing, unless you *live it.* It's yours to lose or yours to glorify. *But don't mourn for me!*

About the Author

Ben D. Mahaffey was born in a small oil boom town in central Wyoming called Midwest, to Roy Ray Mahaffey and Bertha Margaret Karman. He and his two brothers, Ray and Charles were orphaned in 1937. He was adopted by his father's brother, Dave Mahaffey.

He has received the following degrees: A.A., Casper College, Wyoming; B.S., Colorado State University; M.S., Ph.D., Texas A&M University. Mahaffey has taught natural resource management, specializing in historic and natural interpretation, at Texas A&M University and Kansas State University.

He has consulted with and taught professional natural resource managers from state and national resource management agencies. He has received the National Fellow Award from the Association of Interpretive Naturalists. He has also received The Medal of Valor from the Safari Club International.

He is a veteran of the Korean War, having served as a Hospital Corpsman in the Navy and served aboard the U.S.S. Boxer. He has been a private consultant to Fortune 500 Companies and he spent four years as a private consultant to the U.S. Army at the Pentagon.

For several years, before retiring and moving to Utah, he was in private business. Mahaffey has received regional and national honors for teaching and research. He is the author of 25 publications in journals and magazines published during the 1960's—1980's. This is his fifth published book of short stories and other accounts. The first four were titled 50 YEARS OF HUNTING AND FISHING, Volumes I—IV. Although similar, this book includes topics other than hunting and fishing.

Hunting and fishing has been a lifetime passion, having done such on four continents, 12 contiguous states and Alaska. However, this volume also contains his philosophy and accounts of history, politics, religion, war stories and life in general.

He has been married to the former Barbara Alice Proud for 58 years. They are the parents of three sons, Mark, Reno, Nevada; Clark, Mesa, Arizona and Scott, Riley, Kansas. He has nine grandchildren. He resides in Vernal, Utah.